THE MAKING OF

Mr Irresistible

LARRY J GOULD

authorHOUSE®

AuthorHouse™ UK
1663 Liberty Drive
Bloomington, IN 47403 USA
www.authorhouse.co.uk
Phone: UK TFN: 0800 0148641 (Toll Free inside the UK)
*   UK Local: 02036 956322 (+44 20 3695 6322 from outside the UK)*

Published by AuthorHouse 09/11/2020

ISBN: 978-1-6655-8000-7 (sc)
ISBN: 978-1-6655-8002-1 (hc)
ISBN: 978-1-6655-8001-4 (e)

To my grandchildren,
Leah, Emmerson, Libby, Camelie, Raphael, Penelope, and Enzo

CONTENTS

PREFACE

I am a successful failure. It would be impossible to add up the number of things I have failed at so far: schoolwork, sport, girlfriends, my driving test six times, crashing cars numerous times, making new friends, being fired from numerous jobs, and more.

The truth is, we are all potential successful failures. It is in our DNA. We make mistakes, we fall down, and it is not always easy to get back up again.

This book takes you on my journey from poverty to prosperity. I was born in the industrial city of Leeds, England, in 1952, into a working-class family. Our house didn't even have a toilet inside.

From great success working in the Soviet Union to moving to the United States, from achieving a spectacular failure to being forced to return to the UK, you will want to laugh; you will want to cry. I have not let failures and setbacks stop me from pursuing my life in irresistible ways.

My story begins with my first disaster at Harehills Infants School.

ACKNOWLEDGEMENTS

This book is dedicated to my lovely, patient, and supportive wife, Michele. Thank you for putting up with me for almost 40 years and especially for the last three years being driven crazy whilst I wrote the book.

To my children, Joshua, Dalya, and Ilan, as well as my sister, Dianne. You have supported me in this endeavour knowing that some of the stories may be difficult to read.

To Levi Welton, without your support and prodding, the book would not have got off the ground. Thank you for the hundreds of hours you spent listening to my dialogue and for pushing me to tell my story with honesty and transparency.

To Janet R Kirchheimer, you are the most amazing writing coach. Encouraging and demanding, you drove me mad to stretch my writing abilities to their limits.

To Lucy Thornton, for the hours you spent proofreading and reproofing the book.

I am grateful to all the colleagues who have worked with me at thebigword Group for the last 40 years. Without you, I would never have achieved my success.

Finally, to my Executive Assistant, Rory Bickerton. Without your help, this book would never have been completed.

CHAPTER 1

The Road to Hell

"You're going to hell," said Linda Malkin. I was five, and it was a brisk morning at the Harehills Infants School in one of the poorest neighbourhoods in Leeds. The headmistress, Miss Carr, made us begin our morning routine: drinking a bottle of whole milk. I hated milk, especially when it was warm, which it always was. I dutifully followed the rest of the children as we crammed into the school hall and waited for Miss Carr to lead us in prayer. She instructed us to close our eyes, then a hundred little voices called out, "We thank God for the milk we are going to drink today through Jesus Christ, our Lord. Amen!"

Linda Malkin, the cleverest girl in my class, leaned over and, with great pleasure, whispered that I was going to hell for praying to Jesus because I was Jewish. I didn't know what hell was, but from the look on her face, I knew I didn't want to go there. For the rest of the day I fretted about it, and by the next morning I was in a panic. Should I say the prayer to Jesus or not? At the last minute, I settled on the perfect solution. If I didn't drink the milk, I wouldn't need to say the prayer. My Jesus milk crisis was resolved.

Unfortunately, my teacher, Miss Fisher, didn't agree. She noticed that I wasn't drinking the milk with the rest of the assembly and was furious that I had committed the heinous crime of "not participating in school assembly with proper decorum and obedience". My mother was summoned to pick me up from school, and as she walked into the headmistress's office, I hung my head in shame. Quiet the entire walk home, I could see our house welcoming me as we turned the corner onto our street.

I would be safe and far away from Miss Fisher, Miss Carr, Linda Malkin, and all the other mean people at school. Before I could run inside, my mother abruptly stopped walking and bent down in front of me. Holding both my hands in hers, she looked me in the eyes, stretched out one of her soft hands, and stroked my chin. In a matter-of-fact voice, she explained to me, "If you don't want to say that prayer, you don't have to. Just mouth it without actually saying it."

The next morning, I successfully pretended to say the prayer and guzzled down the milk as quickly as possible to get it over with. Life returned to normal. Years later, I realised that the true nourishment I received that day wasn't that dreaded warm milk and prayer, but the lesson from my loving mother. If you think that you only have option A or B, remember to look for option C.

Until the age of three, I lived on Amanda Street, a street crammed with back-to-back terraced houses that had been built in the late 1800s for factory workers. But most of the factory workers were gone, and in their stead were some of the poorest families in all of Leeds. Most of the men were unemployed. I'll never forget having to brave the frigid winter evenings with my mother to use the outdoor toilet, an outhouse in the yard at the back of the house. When I close my eyes, I can still see all of us motley kids playing tag in the cobbled streets while tattered laundry hung on lines, draped high in the air above us.

When I was three, the City Council moved my family from

Amanda Street into a new area of social housing in Ramshead Gardens in Seacroft. This was a huge upgrade, and I felt like we had moved into a palace. We now had an indoor toilet and a bath.

Although we were poor, my parents never stopped trying to provide for my older sister, Dianne, and I. My mother worked as a secretary at the Kraft factory which made cheese slices and my father at the local clothing factory as a foreman. But they could barely make ends meet, and we lived pay packet to pay packet. I don't know how my father found the time, or the money, but he attended night classes and became a chiropodist.

A typical evening consisted of him returning home from the factory, exhausted, and eating alone. He became irritable if we ate with him. After stuffing a few bites into his mouth, the knocks on the door would begin, and our home would be invaded by a procession of old ladies with ugly feet. They'd crowd into our tiny living room, huddle on the sofa, and wait impatiently for my father to take off their shoes, cut their nails, and remove their hardened skin and old-lady corns. The sweaty stench was unbearable, and I would run to my room to get as far away as possible. (To this day, I can barely look at feet.)

If it hadn't been for my grandparents, I would have thought that this was as good as life got. Twice a month, and sometimes more often, my sister and I would be whisked away from Ramshead Gardens. I would go to my mum's parents and my sister to my dad's parents. My grandfather Cross was a retired optician and jeweller, and my grandmother, whom I called Nana Cross (their names, not their dispositions), lived in a clean and comfortable house in a nicer part of Leeds. It looked different, smelled different, had different furniture, and was huge. They even had enough money to invite guests over.

I remember my grandparents' dinner parties where I'd walk around and politely shake hands with all these friendly people adorned with jewellery. Even at the age of six, I knew that a young boy from my neighbourhood didn't belong in the social world my grandparents inhabited.

Within a couple of years, my father began making a little money from all those ugly feet. He was now able to get us new clothes each year for the three major Jewish holidays, Rosh Hashanah, Yom Kippur, and Pesach. Most of the kids in Seacroft only got hand-me-downs or, if they were lucky, new whitsy clothes at Whitsuntide. In hindsight, I realise how much of an outcast this made me feel. Too poor for one neighbourhood and too posh for the other. I didn't belong anywhere.

There were good people who called Ramshead Gardens their home. My next-door neighbour Mrs Cogill comes to mind. Whenever I walked by her house and looked over at her always-half-opened curtains, she'd smile and wave to me. She wore bright red lipstick, had long, wavy blonde hair, and looked like a film star. Plus, she was popular! Every day, dozens of male friends stopped by to visit, yet she always made sure to interrupt her conversations with them to call out and wish me a good day or something kind. Then one day my sister told me that she was a tart. But that didn't mean anything to me—I thought she was sweet, kind, and simply glamorous!

But the woman who really stole my heart was Miss Silver, a teacher who came into my life when I turned six years old and first went to cheder (Hebrew Bible school). Every day when classes ended at Harehills Infant school, I'd sit on a bench in the hall and rock my feet back and forth as I waited for Dianne to collect me. At 3:45pm, we didn't have to ride the bus for 30 minutes, then walk for 20 minutes back home to Ramshead Gardens—we'd get on the "Jewish bus", which was a private bus that took the Jewish kids to cheder.

I didn't know it then, but the real reason my mother sent us to cheder was not for a religious education but because she didn't want us coming home from school to an empty house. She worked late during the week, and cheder was cheaper than paying for a babysitter. But all I cared about was how grown-up I felt getting on the bus with the older kids, holding on tight to my sister as we hit bumps in the road, and being welcomed with tea and biscuits when we arrived. Tea with milk in it. Warm milk, again.

After gobbling up the biscuits and slurping down the tea, we'd begin our Hebrew lessons, which went on all the way until 5:15pm. When cheder finished, there were no buses running nearby to take us home, so we walked through Harehills to a faraway bus stop. But we didn't go alone. The cheder sent a couple of the sixteen-year-old boys from the oldest class as our escorts.

Most of Hebrew school was a pedagogy in misery for me. The head teacher was a crotchety old rabbi with a long grey beard, who I swear looked like he was old enough to have actually witnessed the giving of the Ten Commandments. He always carried a ruler. He never measured anything with it, but if I nodded off ... BAM! My knuckles would burn from the swift sting of his ruler. Those times that I stayed awake but mispronounced any Hebrew words, his hands shot out, he twisted my ears, and I screamed in pain. If I said something disrespectful, SMACK ... his ruler shot out and found my backside. Was Hebrew school hell a requirement to make it to heaven?

But one day, an angel appeared in the form of a new assistant teacher who was brought in midterm to teach us Hebrew reading and writing. Her name was Miss Silver, and she was stunningly beautiful, with a sing-song lilt to her voice and an elegance to her mannerisms. Plus, she gave us chocolate KitKats.

I quickly fell in love with her. Four months later, our class found out that she had become engaged—to the Chief Rabbi of Belgium, no less. I was devastated. My six-year-old heart was broken.

Then my mother was diagnosed with multiple sclerosis.

Up until now, my biggest troubles were being a poor, ethnic minority from social housing. Miss Silver was leaving, and the one source of light and strength in my life was snuffed out in a single diagnosis. My mother was 28 years old. Her doctor told her she would be dead in less than ten years.

My mother refused to disclose her disease to me and my sister; and when I began asking her why she had started shuffling around the house in obvious pain, she replied in a tired voice, "I have weak legs." I tried to fix her the only way I knew how, with hugs and kisses. But she still wouldn't get any better. It wasn't until I was fourteen that I learned my mother had multiple sclerosis, when I asked the family doctor, Dr Hyman, what was wrong with her.

As her condition deteriorated, life in our home began to spiral out of control. She could no longer work, and my father valiantly tried to deal with our drastically worsening financial issues while simultaneously trying to console a wife whose physical ailments would only worsen over time. Before the diagnosis, she used to argue regularly with my father over this, that, and the other, but now she just gave up on it all. His once cheery wife was now reclusive, depressed, and withdrawn. Slowly, my father began to unravel as well.

He began to snap into fits of violence, usually directed at me. Anything could set him off. Speaking too loudly, spilling sauce on the table, turning on his radio, touching his vinyl records; almost anything warranted a sharp smack across the face. During this time, hordes of ugly feet kept swarming through our home, but I now welcomed them as a respite from my father's more frequent attacks.

My parents' relationship swiftly fell apart. My mother became anti-religious and began to defy God as if this was a last resort to assert some semblance of control over her life. Post diagnosis, she often refused to light the Friday night Shabbat candles, and this really drove a wedge between them. The straw that broke the camel's back was when my mother refused to attend the synagogue for the Yom Kippur services with us. The result was that my dad lost his temper and lashed out at me.

Sometimes when I had committed a minor offence like spilling my drink or making a mess on the table, my father would lose it, hitting me until he was out of breath. I still remember looking up from the kitchen floor as my father held me down with one hand, his eyes bulging with rage, as my mother called out weakly from the living room, "Not his head, Julian! Not his head!"

My mother was my guardian angel, my protector. After he'd hit me, I'd flee to my room, and I'd hear her fiercely defending me to my father. As I cowered under the bed covers, I could easily hear his voice reverberate through the thin walls (hers, too weak to be audible), "You always take his side! You always make this out as if I'm being the bad one!" Then he'd storm out of the house in a huff. I'd wrap my arms around my pillow and cry.

What made this worse was that my father wasn't always the bad guy. He actually acted very lovingly towards me sometimes. It was as if there was an on-and-off switch that would flip, and he'd lash out. My sister would warn me, "Don't answer him back, Larry. He won't hit you if you don't answer him back." Her advice never registered, as I needed to convince myself that I wasn't a victim. I had to answer him back. It proved to me that I was strong. After all, I was the only child I knew who could transform my handsome and charming father into a raging father. Maybe this made me feel powerful.

But underneath this six-year-old psychological façade, was a festering well of guilt. What if my sister was right? What if the abuse was all my fault? What if I was responsible for the dark clouds that had enveloped our home? Yet, I couldn't bring myself to admit he was a bad daddy. After all, he showered his affection upon me in his own way, through his love of sport; a love I really didn't share with him at all. "You're coming to the rugby match with me." "OK Daddy." I hated sitting in the freezing cold stadium and had no interest in the game of rugby.

My father was muscular, athletic, a real man's man. I wasn't like him. I couldn't catch a ball to save my life. He even offered to pay me if I caught the ball. I was the boy who'd rather spend a day having tea with my mother and talking about what she would buy me if we went shopping. Yet I'd go with him to the rugby games every Sunday in the dead of winter. All I wanted was to not be scared of him.

I'll never forget how freezing it was in the stadium. Thank God for my dad's friend, Marian Tuff, who at the games would let me sip some of her hot coffee as we huddled in the stands trying to stay warm in our winter coats. After each match, we'd sit at the dinner table, and he'd want to talk about the game. "We saw the great Lewis Jones. That match was magnificent, right son?" "Yes, Daddy. It was lovely!" I knew he wanted to spend time with me, knew he wanted to talk with me, and knew that he was incredibly disappointed in me. All this guilt, sadness, and disappointment finally became too much, and cracks in my psychic armour began to appear.

Migraines. Throbbing pain crushing my skull, knives piercing through my eyes. As my mother's condition got worse, my migraine attacks grew worse as well. When she stopped being able to walk, my migraines got so bad that my father had to take me to hospital. The doctors referred me to specialists who referred me to more specialists. During those months of being shuttled between various clinics and testing sites, the beatings at home continued.

As the concern for my mother's health consumed me, I began to regularly wake up in the middle of the night convinced that she had died. This usually triggered a migraine, and I'd curl up in pain as images of my mother lying dead haunted my imagination. One night, I couldn't take it anymore and tiptoed over to my mother's room, slipped in, and leaned over her bed to make sure she was still breathing. From out of nowhere, my father yanked me out by my elbow. His nostrils flared as he glared at me and demanded to know why I was bothering Mummy while she was sleeping. I stammered, afraid he was going to hit me, and muttered something about not being able to sleep because I was having another one of my headaches.

My father's breathing slowed, his grip on my arm softened. Then he scooped me up in his arms and carried me back to my bed. As he tucked me in, he pressed his hands on my eyes and began massaging them. I felt the migraine go away. When he stopped massaging, the pain returned, and I groaned. Quickly, he returned to massaging and, as I felt the pain wash away, my father whispered in my ear, "My hands are absorbing the pain. Lie back and relax to the sound of my voice. Hmmmmmm, Hmmmmmmm. Oooh, Larry, I just felt the pain coming out of your body and into my hands. Hmmmm. Hmmmm. Now your body can relax, and you can drift off to a peaceful sleep."

For hours, he sat there with me, cradling me in his arms. I eventually fell asleep to the sound of his voice and those big, warm hands caressing my face. When I awoke, it was not just the pain in my eyes that felt more manageable.

Eventually, the doctors prescribed phenobarbital which took away the migraines. But the pills made me constantly drowsy, so drowsy that I had to get a doctor's note allowing me to nod off during class. While the medication may have helped reduce the pain from the migraines, the nodding off during class made me the butt of cruel taunts and bullying.

I was eight-years-old and, once again, I felt like I didn't belong.

CHAPTER 2

Ice Cream

"You can't always get what you want." – The Rolling Stones

With my life falling apart at home and school, I *needed* some goodness in my life. And in my eight-year-old universe, that meant ice cream. Every day, the ice cream van would roll down Ramshead Gardens chased by every kid in our neighbourhood. My sister and I would join the swarm of outstretched hands as we pushed ourselves to the window to speak with his Holiness, the King of all Kings, the ice cream man.

"'Cuse me sir?"

"Yes, lad. What do you want?"

"Can I get that one? It looks amazing!"

"Sure, that's a sixpence cone."

"Uh … uh … do you have anything else?"

A hush fell over the other kids. Nobody, not even the most deprived kids from my poor neighbourhood, ever asked for anything less than a sixpence cone. Even though my parents were relatively better off than most other families, they were stringent with their money and would only let us have fourpence cones. It's ice cream, for God's sake! How could you go cheap on ice cream? But, day after day, I had to watch the other kids gulp down their delicious sixpence cones while my sister and I slunk away with our fourpence cones as everybody nodded sympathetically.

I needed that sixpence cone and soon hatched a plan. My grandparents bought me a comic book every week that I treasured and kept in my room. I had read them all (multiple times!) but, for a large cone, I began selling them.

"Knock Knock!"

"Yes, boy, what do you want?"

"I've got comics on sale for a penny. Would you like one?"

I got a lot of rejections. But, in my mind, I could already see the ice cream melting all over my hands, could already feel the creamy, cold sixpenny taste fill my cheeks as I gulped it down my throat.

As soon as I sold enough comics, I grabbed my sister by the hand and dragged her to wait for the ice cream van, twelve pennies jiggling in my pockets. As it turned the corner onto our street, I raced towards it, and barrelled through the crowd of kids to the front of the line. As soon as the ice cream man opened his mouth to ask what I wanted, I blurted out, "Two sixpenny cones ... with chocolate sprinkles!" As he filled the cones, my eyes sparkled; and when I returned victoriously to my sister with two towering ice cream cones topped with sprinkles, I felt something I hadn't felt in a long time. I was proud of myself.

The only other time in my life I would feel this similar sense of pride was when I drove down the street for the first time in my Bentley. And, even then, it didn't come close to those sixpenny cones! It wasn't a braggadocious pride, but rather an inner pride that quietly affirmed for me one simple truth: your past does not need to determine your future. When the world doesn't give you the reality you want, you can go out and change it. An eight-year-old kid realised that, with persistence, anything is possible. That was the moment I became a businessman.

From then on, I ransacked the house for anything I could sell around my neighbourhood. I took, ok stole, broken pieces of costume jewellery, a box of embroidered handkerchiefs my sister had been given as a present and even a half full bottle of aftershave which I watered down and still managed to sell.

Having my own money was tantalisingly new to me and seduced me into breaking into a bank to get more. Before you judge me, it's not exactly the way you think. Every week we had to bring in a shilling (12 pence) to school, and our teacher Miss Burton, would deposit it into the Yorkshire Penny Bank under our names. Around the same time as my ice cream victory, I had 10 shillings in my bank account which was a nice amount of money in 1960. My parents' entire monthly rent was 27 shillings.

One morning, I was thinking about how my ice cream funds were getting low, and had the brilliant idea of going to the Yorkshire Bank and cashing out all my money. Even though I was only eight, I could easily do it. Every Monday morning, my mother gave me my bank book and one shilling to give to my teacher who wrote the amount in the book and gave it back to me to give to my mother for safe keeping. The school secretary would take the money to the bank. One Friday afternoon, when there was no cheder, I stopped at the Yorkshire Penny Bank and withdrew 10 shillings, enough for 20 sixpence ice creams. I felt like a king. The following Monday, I brought in my bank book and shilling. Miss Burton saw the little blue withdrawal receipt the bank teller had given me, and her eyes widened in shock.

"Laurence, what happened?" She didn't call me Larry, I knew she was mad.

"Well, I took out my money."

"Why did you take out your money?"

"Because I wanted to buy some things."

"What things?"

"Umm … ice cream."

When I arrived home, my mother was livid. The teacher had called her and, even though the money was under my name, Mum acted like I had committed fraud. "That money was for you to have, not for you to spend!" She sent me to bed without dinner and forbade me from having any ice cream for a month. I received my first lesson about the consequences of mismanaging money. But for that week, before I had been caught, I was rich and the ice cream king. It was so worth it.

To this day, I still think of my investments not as "my money to spend" but "my money to have" for a later time. The dramatic way my mother disciplined me impressed upon me the value of honesty that has shaped the way I have always done business. Once again, I learned a lesson about financial transparency from my mother who was trying to teach me to be honest and the consequences if I wasn't.

Ice cream shenanigans aside, I had tasted success with my comic book sales and stolen goods, and it was sweet. Although elements of British society looked down upon me as "that eight-year-old poor kid from the Council Estate", I didn't buy into it because my mother constantly whispered words of encouragement and prophecies of my success into my ears. "Larry, you're such a go-getter. You have such personality. You could charm the birds off the trees Larry."

Even though most of my human interactions at this point were less than satisfying, I think the nurturing adoration of my mother created a loving cocoon against the abuse of my father and the labels of some of society. She refused to let any of what was happening in my life dictate my self-worth.

Additionally, I was whisked away from the tense and stressful existence at home into the clean, bright "palace" of my grandparents. They fed me a constant stream of compliments and, during their regular social get-togethers, I became the centre of attention. The men would mill around the dining table, enjoying the party, and the ladies would wear the most delicious-smelling perfumes as they bent down to squeeze my cheeks. My grandmother taught me the art of complimenting her guests. I remember on one occasion, she told me I must shake hands with everybody and tell everyone it was nice to see them and also mention to Mrs Ansbacher how lovely her perfume smelled. Pretty soon, I felt more comfortable with adults than with children my own age. I couldn't wait to grow up and show the world what I could do.

In 1963, I graduated from junior school and began Stainbeck Secondary Modern School. It was here that I made a new friend who taught me a very important lesson.

On my first day at Stainbeck, I awoke to see a brand new pair of grey trousers draped over the chair next to my bed. Not the short trousers I was used to wearing but a distinguished looking pair of long trousers. I immediately realised that my father had made them at the factory as a surprise gift for me. I slipped them on and felt as grown-up as an eleven-year-old could feel. My legs would certainly be warmer in the harsh English winter, and maybe this would be the moment when my life would finally change for the better.

And change it did.

My migraines got no better, there was hardly a week that would go by without attacks and the strong medication wasn't always working effectively. My father who was still abusive without much provocation also continued to spend many nights pressing his warm hands into my eyes and talking in a calm voice which reduced the panic and pain I felt. The problem was that whilst the drugs did alleviate the pain, it caused me to be very sleepy.

The teachers were indeed sympathetic, in my second year at high school, I was either asleep or foggy which of course made me an oddity to the rest of the pupils. They either kept away from me or made my life a misery. Taunting me and calling me dozy Gould! I suppose I survived because I could actually be present through all of this but also managed to numb myself. There were times of course when I took advantage of the situation especially when it came to football practice.

My father always came with me to my hospital appointments and tried his utmost to be jolly, but I was always terrified at the hospital, even though I was familiar with the building as over the years, I had visited my mother on numerous occasions. At this appointment Dr Alibone took my hand and told me that they were going to do a special test called an EEG which measures what is going on in the brain. I was terrified as my head was connected to electrodes that were attached to my scalp and I held my father's hand very tightly. After a while the machine was turned off and I was told to wait outside. I sat with my father who was still holding my hand but hardly spoke. After what seemed a long time, he was called in to see the Doctor without me.

He came out, his eyes glistening, he hugged me very tightly. I never asked what he said and we headed home. Strangely enough my mother was at the door when we arrived back. She didn't acknowledge me and said "Well Julian, what did he say." He replied, "He is definitely not epileptic." She burst out crying and hugged both of us. I was scared by this reaction and asked what the matter was. My mother replied, "Nothing, it's all great, no more hospitals, no more medication and no more sleeping in class." My migraines, continued for many years, actually until I got married, but my sleeping on the job was over.

Stainbeck Secondary Modern boys' school had a strong macho streak. I kept my love for ballet to myself. Another change was that students were addressed by their surnames, so I went from being called "Larry" to "Gould".

But the kicker (pun intended!) was the hyper focus that this all-male school had on sport. I could have got by if the school was into swimming, which I enjoyed, but the culture was exclusive to rugby, football, and cross-country running. I hated all of these sports. Out of the sixty kids in the running class, my new friend Lawrence Brenner and I would always finish the outdoor course last. Well, close to last. The fat kids were right behind us.

One day, as we were lacing up our running shoes, Brenner turned to me.

"Hey Gould!"

"Yeah Brenner?"

"I have this idea."

"Okay?"

"You know how there's a bus that runs along the cross-country route?"

"Yes …"

"Let's hop on the bus and skip most of the running course. We'll get off a couple of stops before the end, and no one will know!"

I immediately loved the idea. As we crossed the finish line among the first ten kids in our class, I thought to myself, "Well, there's a first time for everything." After we showered and made it back to class, we were told we had been summoned to the office of the headmaster. As Brenner and I opened the door, we saw our coach standing there with the headmaster. Obviously, we were going to be congratulated on our rapid improvement. Then I noticed the headmaster was holding a long, wooden cane.

Our smiles evaporated as the headmaster told us we were going to be caned for two reasons. The first was that we had cheated. The second because we had been stupid enough to make it obvious by coming in with the first ten kids. As he bent us over, and I felt the stinging whip of the cane on my backside, I tried desperately not to cry. Then he stopped and demanded to know if it was my idea to take the bus and skip ahead. To my everlasting shame, my lips shook as I pointed a finger at Brenner. Immediately, the headmaster whacked my only friend in school with the cane six additional times. But the look in Brenner's eyes in that moment when I ratted him out stung me more than the wooden cane ever could.

Remarkably, I retained my friendship with Brenner, and we remained friends until 2018 when he passed away from cancer. I still deeply regret snitching on my friend. What I really learned that day was the number-one rule for maintaining quality long-term relationships: never break your friend's trust in you. If you do, you will suffer that pain for the rest of your life.

CHAPTER 3

The Worst Bar Mitzvah in the History of Leeds

'm not bashing education or academia. On the contrary, doing well in academia opens many doors and the academic education one receives can truly be transformative. But too often, society looks at those who leave school early as outcasts and failures instead of potential disruptors, innovators, and entrepreneurs. If I hadn't dropped out of school at 15, I don't think I'd be where I am today.

I was twelve and a half years old, getting slightly better grades in school and I was hanging out with Brenner who was my best friend. We were now back in our spot at the rear of the cross-country field. I still loved sweets and ice cream, and on a few occasions told my Mum that I lost my bus fare so I could get more money to indulge my addiction. That meant I had to walk three miles to get home but, as they say, "nothing in life worth having comes easy". But as expected, as soon as my mum found out, I got the honesty and integrity speech! This time it did the trick, and I promised her I'd be better. After all, my Bar Mitzvah was just around the corner and what better man could I be than a man of his word. It didn't stop me from wishing that my life would get a little sweeter though.

About three weeks after the honesty and integrity speech, my father came home from the factory in a jolly mood. He told us that he had heard about a house in a better neighbourhood called Alwoodley that we might actually be able to afford to buy. I was *so* happy! We were finally going to move from a Council House to a private home. Although it was completely irrational, a part of me believed that if we moved, everything would change for the better. Mum would get better, Dad would stop hitting me, my migraines would stop, and it would be the beginning of a new life.

Dad turned to my fifteen-year–old-sister, who was about to take her O-level exams, and dating her high school sweetheart and said, "The only problem is that if we move to this house, we won't be able to make a wedding for you, certainly not for many years." In those days, it was tradition in England for the girl's parents to pay for a wedding.

Dianne was a top student in her class and had been dating for some time. She argued with my Dad, wanting both. So he retorted, "Okay Dianne, we're going to leave it up to you to make the choice, and the choice is: our family can move into a new home or we can pay for your wedding. But if you want both the wedding and the family to have a new home, you'll have to go to work and forget about becoming a teacher." She ran into the kitchen, and I followed, begging her to let us move. It was selfish for me to put this pressure on my sister, but all I could see was the new house and my new future.

Dianne left school to work as a clerk for British Gas so she could save up for her wedding, allowing us to begin plans to move. Perhaps she also hoped life would change if she could get Mum and all of us into a better home. But looking back at it now, I didn't realise that it would be the end of her educational aspirations. She was always the most academic in the family and could have gone on to any of the top universities, but she gave it up for love. Placing the weight of the decision on a fifteen year old was not the right thing to do; but it was her sacrifice that finally got us off the Council Estate. It would take us a few months to move out, and it took her almost six years to save up enough money to marry, but she finally wed her boyfriend when she was twenty-one-years old and their union produced two beautiful children, James and Hannah.

Now that we were moving, I imagined my upcoming Bar Mitzvah celebration might also get an upgrade. I had already been to some of my Hebrew School classmates' Bar Mitzvah parties and had an idea of the standards for this coming of age ceremony. But my first let down came when my parents told me they wouldn't be sending out invitations in order to save money.

"No invitations?! Are you kidding me?!"

"Larry, it'll be OK. We'll just invite people when we see them in person and Mum will telephone the others," announced my dad.

I bit my tongue about the invitations and asked my parents about the party. They pushed off the conversation, and I began to get nervous. Then, a miracle happened. My Uncle Cyril, who lived all the way across the pond in America, had sent me a letter congratulating me on my upcoming Bar Mitzvah. As I opened the letter, a cheque fell out. Seconds later, I was running through the house to find Mum as I yelled, "$500! Uncle Cyril sent $500!!" My dad and I went back to the Yorkshire Penny Bank and converted the cheque into pounds to put into my account on the proviso that this time, I couldn't withdraw anything without their permission.

That amount of money was a fortune in 1965, the most money I'd ever seen or had in my entire life. Even before my mum could digest the numbers on the cheque, I was imagining the shock my classmates would have when they would see the luxurious Bar Mitzvah party I would host! But I was let down again as she solemnly told me, "This should be money you have, not money you spend." As I stood before her, crestfallen, she told me they would save the money in an account for me to use when I needed it. Then things got worse.

The invitations had been axed and, when the caterer told my parents that a nice party for 80 guests would cost £500, they axed that as well.

"What can we get for £100?"

"Well, you can do a buffet at the synagogue hall for that amount. But usually, families do more for a Bar Mitzvah."

"No, that's fine. We'll just have the buffet. Thank you."

I was consumed with embarrassment. I was the only kid not to have invitations sent out, and I was the only kid not to have a party, just a pathetic buffet in the synagogue. I am ashamed to say that I forgot the most important aspect of my Bar Mitzvah. Even though I rarely attended synagogue services, I knew I would have to get up in front of everyone and chant the Hebrew prayers. Instinctively, I reached for my ears.

As I rubbed my ears and thought of the rabbi and all the times I mispronounced the prayers in cheder, I became terrified. The fear only grew as we counted down the days until the ceremony. My father had a beautiful suit made for me in the factory, but even that didn't cheer me up. I avoided talking about it with Brenner and hung my head every time someone asked about it. I never thought that perhaps my mother didn't want to spend money on a religious event because of her anti-religious sentiments, or perhaps my parents couldn't afford it. I was so consumed with dread that everything else seemed less significant: my mother's declining health, even my father's beatings.

Finally, the big day arrived. As I arrived at the synagogue with my parents and sister, I nervously plucked at my new suit. I was terrified. Would I be able to chant the prayers? How would my mum get up the stairs to the ladies gallery? She was so weak and could barely walk. I'll never forget watching my father pick her up in his arms and carry her up to the ladies gallery. Until the day before, I was unsure she would be able to come.

My Bar Mitzvah was held in an Orthodox synagogue where men and women sit and pray separately. My mum would sit in the ladies gallery with my sister, Nana Gould and Nana Cross and be able to look down to watch the proceedings. As my dad tenderly placed her into a seat, I wanted to stay with her and hide. But, I followed my dad downstairs to the men's section of the sanctuary and looked up at her. She was wearing the biggest pink hat in the world. She looked at me with her pale face and smiled. I felt like I was underwater looking up at everyone, but I somehow managed not to pass out.

Traditionally, the rabbi of our synagogue would say nice things at the end of the service about the Bar Mitzvah boy and his family. But, of course, the rabbi wasn't there that day. He had to be at another Bar Mitzvah in the more prosperous part of the city. I stumbled through the prayers, and we couldn't have left the synagogue soon enough. I was only allowed to invite Brenner to the buffet. After the buffet, we went to lunch at a restaurant called The Vintage Steak Bar. But none of my grandparents were invited because my parents told me, "We have to save money." Yes, Mum let me have ice cream at the restaurant but it did little to assuage the trauma of having the most joyless Bar Mitzvah in the history of Leeds.

But one good thing did happen. Out of all the presents I received, the best one came from my father. He stopped hitting me. I am not sure why. Maybe it was because at 13, I had become a man.

Another big change after my Bar Mitzvah was that I became financially responsible. I didn't win the lottery or get a lucrative weekend job. Rather, after we counted up the £70 I had collected in gifts, my father told me bluntly that now I was responsible for buying my own clothes and paying for my own holidays. He said, "You have a bank account with £250 in it." Both my parents knew how miserable I felt about my Bar Mitzvah and tried to convince me that I was lucky because I had ended up with all this money in the bank while the other kids who splurged on a party ended up with nothing. I wasn't convinced.

I now think no matter where you are financially in your life, the key to happiness is finding a way to have fun. Not to show off to your friends the way I was thinking of for my Bar Mitzvah, but rather to create a milestone. Whether it's a birthday, graduation party, or even a wedding, milestones are priceless. Since my Bar Mitzvah I have lived by the creed "Celebrate everything!", and I think it's my way of trying to make it up to that thirteen-year-old kid who never got to have the celebration he was hoping for.

When I think about my Bar Mitzvah, I believe that a small buffet would have been good enough for me if it had been arranged in a joyous way. In fact, just having a big cake and all my family and friends around me would have been better than what I experienced. I think my parents and I missed the point: it is about the joy you put into a milestone event, even if it's one cake that makes the celebration with the people you care about.

About six months before my 40th birthday, I got the surprise of my life. My wife, Michele, told me I had to get ready for a special party. I kissed her without even asking what was so special about it as my birthday was five months away. But she wanted to talk seriously and sat me down. Her green eyes lit up as she told me, "I know you never got to have a proper Bar Mitzvah. I'm going to make you a Bar Mitzvah for your 40th birthday the way it should have been, the way it could have been, and the way you deserve."

Here I was, a father of 3 small kids, and still terrified at the thought of having to chant the prayers aloud in the Etz Chaim synagogue in

Leeds by myself in front of my family and friends. Nevertheless, Michele made sure the excitement and joy only grew as we counted down the days until the ceremony. I had a beautiful new suit made for me.

Once again, my mum and father were there. But this time, 27 years later, my mum walked in on her own two feet and, as she looked at me with a healthy, rosy colour in her cheeks, I couldn't control myself and rushed to embrace her. I was so overcome with joy that everything else seemed insignificant. My wealth, my work, even my turbulent childhood and relationship with my father.

In 1997, when I was 45, I was approached by an executive from the United Jewish Israel Appeal (UJIA) who told me of the sad plight of Ethiopian Jews who were suffering terrible hardships after being airlifted to Israel. As thousands of families arrived with only the clothes on their back and the few items they could carry, they were placed in absorption centres, given clothes, and a small amount of money on which to subsist.

I visited an absorption centre in the north of Israel where the Ethiopians were temporarily living in caravans and was thrilled to tell them that UJIA would fund their Bar/Bat Mitzvah celebrations. The first year, 16 boys and nine girls made the four hour journey to celebrate at The Great Synagogue in Jerusalem followed by a festive lunch. We were honoured that the Chief Rabbi, Rabbi Lau would address the children at their ceremony. We took the children and their family members, over to the Haas Promenade with its view of the old city and then to the Western Wall where we had arranged for a band to play music so these families could sing and dance together. In the past 24 years, over 600 Ethiopian boys and girls have celebrated their milestone rite of passage with joy.

CHAPTER 4

High School Drop Out

After my thirteenth birthday, my relationship with my father was still difficult, but at least he wasn't physically abusing me anymore. His outbursts now only consisted of him screaming and hurling insults at me. We finally moved to our new home in Alwoodley, a suburb of Leeds and one of the best neighbourhoods in all of West Yorkshire. "Thank God for all those ugly feet and my sister," I whispered as I surveyed the area into which we were moving. I felt such relief to move into a home where I felt I belonged.

But the upheaval of the move was too much for Mum, and she had a nervous breakdown. For a year, she would barely leave the house. She cried all the time. If things hadn't improved at my new school, I don't think I would have been able to handle it. I was finally beginning to make new friends.

I had begun to discover a passion for writing and acting. School plays, acting in The King and I, keeping a journal, writing articles for the school magazine, you name it. I was signing up and getting involved. Dad would have preferred that I had signed up for the rugby team, but Mum was happy that I was happy. Even with her problems, she still made sure I knew how proud she was of me.

As the year progressed, things got better. My sister became the leader of the local Jewish youth club, B'nai B'rith. My parents made her drag me along. Not so cool for her, but she took me, and it changed my life. B'nai B'rith's focus was on charity, volunteering, socials, and cultural events, and I was delighted when I discovered how many friends I could make. I am sure it must have helped that Dianne was the leader. The first B'nai B'rith event she brought me to was a dance in a barn near our new house. Apart from my sister and a couple of her friends, I knew nobody there.

But I was immediately approached by a girl called Sharon Walden who would become one of my closest friends. She started talking to me. She was very friendly and outgoing and introduced me to her crowd of friends. It was a magical evening, and I was deliriously happy. Not many of these kids were from my school and, it made me more relaxed. Most of my new B'nai B'rith friends came from affluent families and went to the top schools in Leeds. I was invited to parties, homes, and the cinema. Thank God, I was now living in Alwoodley; I would never have been invited if we had still lived in a Council House.

One of the things I particularly enjoyed was the volunteer work we did. Every week, a group of us would go to MenCap House and help with the kids, many of whom had Down Syndrome or other handicaps. During one of these volunteer outings, my friends began talking about which careers they might want to go into: law, medicine, accountancy, banking, that sort of thing. When they asked me what I wanted to do, I didn't have a good answer. I was only getting average grades in school and really didn't have any interest in higher academics. But the real reason I didn't have an answer was that Uncle Cyril's funds were running out, and I didn't think my parents would pay for me to go to university. My friends resumed their animated conversation about the pros and cons of Oxford vs. Cambridge.

One day there was a job fair at school and in three neighbouring booths stood representatives from the UK's biggest department stores, Lewis's, Schofield's, and Debenhams. I was very flattered when all three of them told me I would be very good in retail and, could take college classes as part of a vocational diploma in retail management. That night I told my Dad I wanted to drop out of school and begin working as a retail apprentice. At first, my Dad was speechless which made me strangely happy. But part of me prayed that he would say no, as I was terrified that I would lose my newly found social standing. It was the kiss of death to start work at 15 and not go to university unless you were a slow learner or very poor, of which now I was neither.

My father duly wrote a note to the school informing them that I would be leaving at the end of the school year. Two days later, he told me that the school had called to invite him to discuss my future as they felt I should continue my education. To be honest, I felt relieved; but I wasn't going to share that with my father. I think a part of me was convinced that he would never let me actually drop out of school.

"So, what'd you tell them, Dad?"

"Well, my dear Lepki, I told them that if my son wanted to work, I would support his decision!"

Now it was my turn to be shocked. I couldn't believe he was actually supporting my idea. Even more surprising was that he called me Lepki, a nickname he only used when he was in a particularly loving mood. Perhaps if I hadn't been so low on my Uncle Cyril funds, I would have changed my mind and told him right then that I wanted to stay in school. But I knew I needed the money, so I thought I had no other choice but to pretend I had no reservations about my decision to drop out. And yes, a big part of me didn't want to give my father the satisfaction of realising my decision was largely a bluff of rebelliousness.

For the last six months of the school year, my decision meant that I was moved to the Transition Form. I had the chance to learn vocational subjects like car maintenance or joinery, among other trades. I chose shorthand and typing.

I had enjoyed one year of making friends and fitting in, but that was now completely eclipsed by the drama of being known as "the soon to be school dropout." I knew I liked writing and felt I needed a skill that would be useful for me in the real world. The plan was that these classes would help me become a journalist. Learning shorthand and typing was something no other boy in my school had ever done. My friends were so shocked at my decision that I had to pretend to be very happy about it. Some friends dropped me immediately. One about to be ex-friend said, "Even male hairdressers wouldn't want to do shorthand and typing!"

Each morning when I would walk into class, the girls would giggle at me. The one good thing about learning shorthand and typing was that I was able to avoid the car maintenance and carpentry classes, which was a bloody relief. There was another good thing about taking that class. My Mum, who had once been a secretary, felt needed as she helped me practise my shorthand and typing at home. We had something more to talk about, and I wanted to brighten her day when I returned home from school.

I had already lost one group of friends and didn't need to lose another, so I conveniently never shared the fact that I was learning shorthand and typing with my friends at B'nai B'rith and focused on talking about the day release programme and taking college classes, rather than the fact I would be working as a sales assistant.

The drama at school continued as the parents of my classmates found out I was dropping out of school to go to work. Again, people were looking down on me. Just as easily as I had been accepted, I was out once again. A few of my classmates tried to remain friends, but that didn't last long. Some were pressured by their parents not to be friends with me as they felt I would be a bad influence on them and distract them from their studies.

While my former classmates were about to begin their summer holidays, I began my first job as a sales apprentice at Debenhams, one of the biggest department stores in the United Kingdom.

In those days, proper business etiquette dictated that even though I was just fifteen, I was no longer referred to by my first name. That would be unprofessional. Once again, what I was known by changed.

Until the age of 11, people called me "Larry".

Throughout secondary school, I was "Gould".

And now, I was "Mr. Gould". It made me feel like a grown up. At fifteen years old and four weeks, I became a working man. I got what I wanted, and I hated it.

CHAPTER 5

Becoming Mr Gould

6ᵗʰ June, 1967. It's a Monday morning and I walk into Debenhams wearing the third new suit my father had made for me. I'm the youngest person on the lighting and gifts team and definitely overeager. The floor manager loves me because she can send me all over the store, and I'll drop whatever I am doing to rush forward to help her.

On my second day at work, the deputy manager in my department sent me to the display department to get a long stand, which I assumed was some kind of display stand. The display department sent me to the fur department. The fur department told me that all the long stands were kept in the dispatch department in the basement. I rushed down the escalator, fell, and cut my knee. I didn't bandage it as I was afraid that I had been out of my department for too long. When I got to the dispatch department, they told me to wait whilst they looked for one. I was very anxious as they kept me waiting for what seemed like an age. Finally they said that I should go back to the lighting and gifts department as they had located one there. I went back to my deputy manager and told him that there was a long stand in the department. My colleagues started laughing, and I had no idea why. "Mr. Gould," my department manager said, "You certainly have had a long stand.

You are the long stand," and he burst out laughing. To my horror, embarrassment, and everlasting shame, I burst out sobbing. I wanted to die. I wanted to go back to school. Whilst it was done in humour, I remember saying to them pathetically, "I didn't think grown-ups were such bullies."

My work colleagues felt badly about what they had done, and pretty soon I got over the drama of my welcome to the department. They began to train me in how to sell products "on the floor". My natural instincts were only half the game. Their training got me to the finish line. I still love selling because they taught me how to structure a sales conversation and gave me the confidence to get on the floor and sell.

At the time, I didn't realise how much the sales training I received would help me in my future career and, indeed, my life. I think more people need to learn and respect the amazing power of practising sales techniques. I recently was the keynote speaker at a conference for the top fifty fastest growing companies in the north of England. I asked the audience of more than 200 executives how many of them were in sales, and only eight raised their hands. Then I asked, "How many of you have opportunities in your work to talk to a client?" They nearly all raised their hands. They were all slightly stunned when I shouted back, "Then you're all in bloody selling – get over yourselves!"

Sales should not be sneered at; it is a valuable skill. I think sales should be a degree one can major in. And I'm not talking about marketing. I find it interesting that so many people talk about having degrees in marketing and a job in marketing, because they are embarrassed to admit that they are in sales. Sales is a demonstrable skill that even the cleverest people aren't learning in their academic pursuits and just as a point of interest, the top earners in many companies are normally the top sales people.

While many of my friends from B'nai B'rith were still three years away from starting university, I was studying a very important skill set: how to deal effectively with people. While my former school peers were studying hard in high school, I was dealing with the frequent rejection that comes with sales. Whilst this rejection was sometimes depressing, I was learning from it and becoming a more effective salesperson. Even today, the majority of the top one hundred richest people in the UK have very few academic qualifications. But they know how to communicate, how to lead, and how to sell.

My first big sale was an expensive chandelier. It brought me so much prestige from some of my co-workers that I walked around for days feeling all cocky and full of myself. Other salesmen noticed and were overtly irritated by my success. Then the customer returned and wanted his money back, something about the chandelier not looking right in his home. I was devastated. Hero to zero in four days. I was depressed and thought I should act more modestly and wait for sales to come to me.

But I swallowed my pride, got up, and tried again. The more attempts I made, the more sales I made. That's why the hardest part of being in sales is not just the pitch, but something far more important: being self-motivated. It's going out to make the sale even when you can't be bothered.

Within a year, my enthusiasm paid off, and I was promoted to manager. Not manager of the store, but manager of the paint and wallpaper department. It was still a big win for me as I was the youngest person at 16 to get a job as a manager. Some of my colleagues were clearly put out by this. I did two things that upset them. I was super enthusiastic, and I only took a twenty-minute lunch break. But the harder I worked, the more successful I became.

And yet, even though I was finally getting ahead, again I felt on the outside. Being 16-years-old, I didn't have enough life experience to connect with my co-workers in the department. Margaret, who was probably in her mid-30s from the Lancôme section, was one of my friends. She'd show me the bruises on her arm she got from her boyfriend. Jim from furniture was 50, and I nicknamed him "Miserable Jim" because he constantly complained about how hard the work was. My best friend at work was another apprentice, Kathy, who worked in lingerie. She told me she had become pregnant and then proceeded to ask me for money for a bottle of gin so she could flush out the baby by drinking it in a hot bath. I asked her if it worked, and she told me, "No, I was sick all night, and I'm still bloody pregnant." (I was secretly in love with her). I'd have a cigarette with the paint and wallpaper team every day at lunch. Although they were kind and supportive, I didn't have much in common with them. At the same time I had less and less in common with my old school friends. The only person I really kept in touch with was Brenner.

A compulsory part of my sales apprenticeship was Day Release, which meant studying for a retail diploma. In addition to working in the store five days a week, and day release on Tuesday, I also had a night class on Wednesday and homework to complete. All I wanted to do was sleep.

But then two things happened that had a very positive effect on my life. I was not into sport, but I did love swimming and so did my father and sister. Every Sunday in the summer, we'd go to the local swimming pool. Of course, my mother couldn't join in and would sit in a deck chair and watch us from afar. One day, my father said to her that he had read an article saying that swimming was good for people with MS, and she should have a try. At first she refused, but my dad lifted her up, took her to the shallow end, and gently immersed her in the water. Over the next few weeks, he took time teaching her how to swim, and by the third week my mum managed to swim the width of the pool. I was glad I was in the water as it hid my tears as I watched her swimming independently. I felt like she had won an Olympic medal. She was so proud of herself and, as she sat on the steps at the shallow end, she said it was the first time in a long time that she felt normal. This was a turning point in my mum's life, and it gave her more confidence for the future.

The second thing was that I fell I love again. Replacing my former love, Miss Silver, was a new girl. She came from a far-away, exotic land. America.

CHAPTER 6

Larry the Loner to Larry the President

When one of my friends or their parents came into the store, I'd duck behind a clothing rack or run into the back room until they were gone. In addition to not telling my B'nai B'rith friends I had dropped out, I also avoided talking with them about my job as a sales apprentice at Debenhams. I was so concerned with how they would judge me: I had dropped out, and I wasn't going to university.

I didn't keep my job at Debenhams a complete secret from my friends. I just avoided talking about it. It was hard because I was actually very proud of my promotion, but too embarrassed to share with them. Instead, I would drop what I was doing into conversation.

"So Larry, what exactly do you do in the store?"

"I'm actually doing a retail programme."

"Really? Which one?"

"Well, it's a specialised diploma in retailing."

"What exactly does that mean?"

"It's pretty simple, actually. Part of the curriculum is hands-on experience in a retail store, and the rest of the time, I'm at college."

Instead of being proud that I had a full-time job, went to Day Release one day per week and took night classes, I hid it. Looking back, I am ashamed that I did but I was 15 and not confident enough around my friends and in myself.

Between work and study and my free time taken by B'nai B'rith, an entire year passed by in the blink of an eye. I was taking my first year exams for my college diploma. After one of my classes, my teacher called me over and told me that I had done so well over the past year that I had the second-highest grade of anyone on the course. I had never been a particularly successful or terrible student. Consistently very average was my academic speed, so this was exciting news for me. As soon as I got home, I waited impatiently for my dad to arrive. After he settled in, I proudly shared the good news. He stroked his chin and looked me up and down.

"And how many other students are there in this class?

"Well, Dad, there are two classes, and each one has about twenty-five students. I'm number two out of both classes!"

"Well, the rest of your classmates must be bloody thick if you came in second."

Mum was very proud.

In the end, I never attended graduation because Mum couldn't get there. I never mentioned the award to any of my friends.

There were two popular Jewish social clubs where I grew up: B'nai B'rith and Habonim. B'nai B'rith, the oldest Jewish service organisation, was founded in 1843 and was not welcoming to people from my social, financial, and educational background. Habonim, a Zionist movement was founded in 1929 in the United Kingdom. After realising how many friends I had made when my sister recruited me to join B'nai B'rith, I also joined Habonim and attended events sponsored by both organisations. Luckily, both societies met on my one day off, Sunday, one in the afternoon, and one in the evening.

I was involved with both groups even though I knew that the kids who were members of one group usually didn't join the other. The B'nai B'rith kids tended to be from more well off families than the Habonim kids. A year before I was elected president of B'nai B'rith, my parents surprised me and told me I could host my birthday party in our new home in Alwoodley. I couldn't believe it and was so beside myself with excitement that I invited every single friend I had from both social clubs.

When the day of the party arrived, I was shocked to see how it played out. Whilst teenagers filled our home, the kids from B'nai B'rith and the kids from Habonim didn't mingle or speak to each other. The B'nai B'rith kids were on one side of the room and the Habonim on the other. As I walked between both groups, each one made critical and demeaning comments about the other. I panicked and didn't know who to talk to or which side of the room to be on. How did I never realise this before?

Although I managed to make it through my party without losing friends on either side, I was relieved when my parents came home. "Mum the kids aren't talking to each other, what do I do?" She replied, "It's your party, dad and I are going to bed." In the UK, just as in most societies, who your friends are often defines you. Yet, because I didn't declare sides, I was able to be friends with a wider circle. The realisation I had on my sixteenth birthday has stayed with me to this very day. Even though I was disappointed with both groups, I managed to stay above the fray and fluctuations of most social politics. It is quite liberating, actually. From then on, I avoided creating a situation where both groups were in the same room.

I was elected President of B'nai B'rith one year after my party, maybe it was my good looks. While my friends were getting more and more locked into their social and career boxes of choice, I had no boxes. I was a worker by day, student by night, and able to easily move between various social groups in the community. To my utter joy, my peers who nominated me were perhaps sending a message that I would have never thought possible: that it was ok to be different, to chart my own path. I had chased acceptance. Now, not only was I accepted, but I had been voted to lead my peers. I told everyone that I didn't care if I won the presidency or not but, of course, I absolutely did.

It remains one of the highlights of my life. I was the first person who had dropped out of school to win the presidency. I had to prepare a speech to give in front of all the members of B'nai B'rith, their parents, alumni, and my family. I was terrified.

Recently, someone from Leeds texted me a photo of a polished wooden plaque that still hangs in Street Lane Synagogue, I gasped when I read the gold leaf letters.

"President - *Laurence J. Gould, 1968-9*"

Unlike the trauma of my Bar Mitzvah, I was now gaining the confidence of being a working man who had recently been promoted, had a good social life, some great close friends, and was bringing home his own money. I launched into my speech with gusto. After I finished, I was swarmed by people shaking my hand and congratulating me. I was shocked to feel a familiar grasp on my shoulder and turned to look into the teary eyes of my father. "Lepki, I am so impressed. You were amazing!"

Time slowed down. The words that people were speaking to me faded into silence. All I could see was a tear streaming down my father's face. I had long ago decided that the only person I needed to be proud of me was me, and, of course, Mum. I didn't want a single tear on my father's face to mean so much to me. But it did. A part of me had been waiting for years, perhaps my entire life for this moment. My father was proud of me. Although this would never make up for the abuse, that one tear became another layer in my psychic armour.

I was now approaching 17 and, in between my various commitments, had started dating. I had three pools of available young women to choose from - B'nai B'rith, Habonim, and the girls at Debenhams. Of course, as a past president I'm obligated to say B'nai B'rith had the best looking girls.

Like most teens, I had trouble in the beginning. I was naturally shy, but what gave me the edge was that I was one of the better-looking chaps in the neighbourhood (if I may say so myself)! A friend of mine once joked that the key to happiness is being good-looking. While it's obviously humorous, there's actually some truth to that statement. I might have been average in many areas of my life, but being above average in the looks department meant I didn't have to work as hard as other boys to attract girls. I think that's part of the reason I became so popular in the social clubs so quickly.

I liked women because my Mum, Nana Cross and my sister had always been nice to me, and I was very close to them. So I was very comfortable talking with girls about a whole array of subjects, although shorthand and typing was one I avoided.

Yet, I started to experience the same problem as before. I didn't fit neatly into a box. Or, rather, I didn't seem to attract girls who fit me. I believed the girls in the social clubs weren't mature enough, and the girls at work were older and didn't want to go out with me because I was too young. My dating life was really choppy in the beginning.

I don't think I was allowing anyone to be truly intimate with me, and I wasn't allowing myself to be intimate with anyone. And for good reason: I was afraid. Afraid of losing it all. After believing I was truly comfortable with not fitting in, I had finally managed to find a way to fit in; and I was desperate not to lose it. I was feeling full of contradictions, popular with the posh kids, president of B'nai B'rith, and simultaneously the newly promoted manager of wallpaper and paint at Debenhams who could be fired at any time. My friends were taking entrance exams for Oxford and Cambridge or other universities and had an idea of what the next four years of their lives would look like. The only security I had was one week – If I didn't perform well at my job or if the store wasn't doing well, I could be made redundant. I always held my breath after Christmas trade and the January sales. The week after the January sales, employees were called to the personnel office and I was terrified I would be called.

Even though I was popular, good-looking, and succeeding across the board, on the inside I was scared. And I think that's why I wasn't initially successful with dating because I was afraid to let anyone inside my mind and heart. It's probably why I ended up having a fling with Kathy, my colleague at work. But the differences in our lives were too many. Plus, I couldn't get the image of her drinking gin in the bathtub out of my mind.

At the last meeting of our youth group before the summer break, a friend of mine brought his cousin along. She was staying with him for a six-week holiday and, from the moment I laid eyes on her, I was besotted. For the first time since Miss Silver, I was in love. This time it was with Sandy, the beautiful girl from that far-away exotic land of America. New Jersey to be exact.

CHAPTER 7

My American Girlfriend

One of the reasons I fell in love with Sandy was because she had this particularly attractive quality. She was American.

The interactions I had with Americans were by watching them on the telly. I was fascinated by their cowboy accents and how they said all these strange things such as bathroom instead of toilet or closet instead of wardrobe. But underneath these charming quirks was this feeling that meeting a real-life American was like meeting a celebrity. It was most likely because I was smitten. Sandy came from this glorious place across the pond where dreams came true, where golden opportunities glittered on every pavement, and words like adventure and pioneer were bandied about.

Conversely, when I eventually moved to the United States in 1973, I experienced the same sort of celebrity status with my English accent. People always wanted to hear the "Queen's English". It has become so in demand that I still consider it a business asset.

But I had another reason to admire America more than the average Brit. My Mum was an American. Her father and mother, Joe and Rebecca Cross, had briefly emigrated to the States to join some family, and during that time my mother was born in Brooklyn. When she was three, they returned to the UK, only because Nana Cross could not bear the humidity of the 1920s New York summers. My mum always had pride in the fact that she was born in Brooklyn, and it was her lifelong ambition to visit the States again. I used to boast about it all the time to the other kids in Leeds. "Yup, my mum is a Yankee like those ones you see on the telly!"

Although we could not afford to travel there, our connection to the States was kept alive by my mother's American cousin, Cyril Marcus. My sister and I called him Uncle Cyril. An eccentric, wealthy New York City businessman, he had married three times, had no children, and always sent gifts for my mother, my sister, and me. He hated my father, and the feeling was mutual. Every Hanukkah, I'd eagerly await the two cartons covered in international stamps and scribbles to arrive. One of them contained navel oranges, a delicacy from his vacation spot in Florida. No one in my neighbourhood had ever seen a navel orange, and its exotic pink-rose flesh was the talk of all the kids who lined up on our step to try a slice. The other carton contained boxes of Barton's Hanukkah chocolates and dreidels which made our holiday truly magical. To see those boxes arrive each year was wondrous.

When I was eight, Uncle Cyril began writing me letters. Every three weeks, another letter would arrive, and I'd hastily write back to my pen pal. I don't remember much of the content from those early days, but it was the beginning of my relationship with him. It instilled in me a fondness for America similar to my mum's. It also might have been his generous birthday gifts or the fact that he never wrote to Dianne.

I think if my mother hadn't been diagnosed with MS, she would have returned to the golden land, the land where the streets were paved with gold. When I was eight we were very excited as my mother had an appointment with the American consulate in Bradford to finalise her dual British/American citizenship, which meant that my sister and I would also be able to receive dual citizenship too. But she was too weak to stay in the queue and had to return home. She never did receive her American citizenship and, of course, neither did we. I was devastated, however, it still didn't stop me from claiming I was half American, which in those days of limited travel was quite a claim.

My father, on the other hand, detested Americans. This was because he had been in the British infantry during World War II and, toward the end of the war, American soldiers started showing up in Leeds. These foreigners arrived with their charming accents, chewing gum, cigarettes, silk stockings, and gleaming white teeth. Also, they were arriving late to the war after the British had done all the heavy lifting and were getting all the girls! As more and more British girls began dating these GIs, fights broke out in the pubs and on the streets, and at one point the American soldiers in Leeds had to be confined to their barracks to keep the peace. My mother and father started dating around this time, and my father was furious when she showed him letters containing marriage proposals from three different American GIs. Actually, my father grumbled for many years that he suspected Mum had chosen to name me Larry, an uncommon name in England, because of her feelings for one of "those bloody Americans".

But there was more to it than just a macho turf war over mating rights. There were some major cultural differences that made the American style of communication jarring for the average Brit. The English were more formal while the Americans prided themselves on being personable and familiar. Even today, I am taken aback when a stranger on the streets of New York City gushes, "*Oh my Gawd, I love your glasses. They're just gorgeous!*" But secretly, I love it. I remember my dad telling me, during the war, when an American would joyfully greet a passer-by on the street with their white teeth, you'd invariably see the English roll their eyes as if to say, "*This is complete bollocks. You don't even know me!"* Uncle Cyril came for a visit with his first wife shortly after the war, and she gave my mum a pair of her silk stockings, which she said she had only worn once! My father was disgusted and told my mum to give them back. "Too personal, too personal," I heard him mutter angrily under his breath.

But it was precisely this personable and free-spirited attitude that attracted me to Sandy like a bear to honey. I couldn't get enough of her. All the girlfriends I had had before would always wait for me to make the first move. And the really good girls would initially object to a guy's advances.

It was completely different with Sandy. She was very open and forthcoming and completely at ease with herself and her body. It was the way she laughed out loud, the way she moved so confidently when we went on our first walk together, the way she made the first move and initiated our first kiss. She was completely uninhibited and happy to share herself in a fun and joyful way.

The weeks flew by that summer. When she returned to America, she was my girlfriend, and we were rationed to one telephone call of three minutes per month and began writing to each other every other day. In her letters, she told me how brave she thought I was for leaving school to go to work, which made me feel a hero. She also filled her letters with compliments that made me feel great about myself. At a time when I was riddled with insecurities and had been keeping my feelings bottled up, she was the fresh air I desperately craved. Over the next four years, we'd reunite in Leeds when she came to visit her family every summer and sometimes during the December school break. For the rest of the time, I had to resort to containing my passion to words and syllables on a page.

Now that I had the girl, I needed the car. When all my friends from B'nai B'rith turned 17, they either had their own car or borrowed one from their parents. Not me. I had taken dozens of driving lessons and multiple driving tests and failed them all. I'm still rubbish at driving.

The thought of picking Sandy up for a date and walking her to the bus stop was unbearable. Although I was doing well in my retail apprenticeship at Debenhams, I began scouring the newspapers for a new job. I had one primary objective: a job that offered a company car. Finally, I saw a furrier job that fit the bill. In the interview, I had to put my selling skills to the test to show them why they should hire me even though I didn't have a driving licence. In those days, there was a waiting list and I didn't tell them I had failed every previous driving test, only said that I'd be taking one in six weeks. They hired me on the condition that I would pass my test. I failed that one as well and spent four months carrying armfuls of fur coats all over Leeds on the bus and train before the truth came out. I was promptly fired.

After five more driving tests, and over one hundred lessons, I finally passed. But I gave up the hunt for a company that offered a car. Instead I got a new job working for ASDA (the British Walmart headquartered in Leeds and one of the largest hypermarkets in Europe at the time) as a management trainee. This was exciting because normally to get into this programme, you needed to have a degree. I was accepted because I had worked as an apprentice for two years at Debenhams. Within six months, I was promoted to manager of the non-foods (clothing, household items, etc.) department in Nottingham. Apparently, it was a combination of my work ethic and the fact that all the managers there had been sacked for stealing. ASDA wanted someone like me to be the new Sheriff of Nottingham. I was in charge of forty staff members. Nottingham was 80 miles away, which meant I had to leave home. I was now 18, terrified, and excited. For the first few weeks, they put me up in a hotel. Then I moved into my own accommodation, sharing a house with two teachers and a musician. Every Friday night from a pay phone, I called my mother to report what my new flat mates were like.

"Um, hi Mum!"

"Hi Larry, how's Nottingham?"

"Well, um, my flat mates are nice but they're always doing … doing drugs."

"Doing what?" her voice rising in a panic.

"They're always getting high, Mum. High off drugs."

"Don't you take any! If you know what's good for you."

"Yes, Mum."

Thankfully, my flat mates didn't have enough time to properly school me in their extra-curricular activities because I was again promoted six months later, and this time I was sent to Edinburgh where I was now the team leader responsible for a team of 50 whose job it was to merchandise and set up non-food departments in a period of three to six weeks. After a successful opening in Edinburgh, I was in charge of setting up new stores around the UK, working 18-hour-days in each new store.

Living away from Leeds improved my relationship with my dad, a bit. With my new job title, he began to give me a little more respect and actually told me how proud he was of me. But his approval no longer mattered.

After nine months. I was promoted to Trainee Buyer based at headquarters back in Leeds. With my promotion came a bump in pay which I promptly used along with the remaining £175 of Uncle Cyril's Bar Mitzvah money to buy my first car, a very used navy blue Ford Anglia which hardly ever started without kicking the damn car and spraying WD40 on the spark plugs. When Sandy came to Leeds for the summer, I was so proud to pick her up in it. But she was afraid of it. Probably because parts of the car kept falling off as we drove or because

I kept bumping into stationary objects. Or maybe it was the engine that conked out randomly throughout the day. I still managed to coax her in, and we had some fun times in that old heap of nuts and bolts.

The letters from Uncle Cyril kept coming. I rarely wrote about my work success. This was not due to modesty, but rather not to draw attention to the fact I had dropped out of school and hadn't been to university. He had been floating the idea for some time now that I should come to America to work for him. I suppose I had always been worried my successful and wealthy Uncle Cyril would be disappointed in me, and I never found the courage to tell him. I still had this hang-up about my scholastic pedigree and a voice inside me said, "How could you accept his offer to work for an American company when you never even got a real University degree?"

So I politely declined his offer, although I told my friends and colleagues that it was my dream to work in America. But it was also true that I was scared of leaving home and flying across the pond. So instead, I decided I needed a new car. Once again, I began hunting for a new job with better pay and a company car. Also, I wanted the chance to save up enough money to make a trip to America to visit Sandy, which was all I could think about.

My next career stop took me to William Warner, a pharmaceutical company, where I was able to parlay my experiences into a better-paying job with a shiny new Ford Estate. My dream came true, it had no bumps or scrapes, at least for the first two weeks. I was in the toiletry and confectionary division focused on products such as cough drops and shampoo. My job consisted entirely of visiting newsagents and chemists across England. But with my hopeless driving, I kept getting lost. So I had to work twice as hard to make my sales and meet my quotas, leaving very early in the morning and arriving back to Leeds late at night.

One of the techniques I discovered that helped was talking to my customers about the benefits of a product and not just its features. For example, in the winter I pushed Halls Menthols. I told customers that they could expect to have at least a 70% increase in sales in the winter if they were placed next to the check-out. Then I would provide them with a stand and often got them to move another product to make space for our brand. The training at William Warner's was fantastic, I was 20 years old and gaining confidence in my ability to think outside the box and sell in ways that other sales people did not.

So when William Warner offered the exorbitant prize of 100 pounds to the salesperson who could place a product in the most unlikely place, I jumped at the opportunity. Because I now had a car and I was somewhat over-spending on my social activities. My colleagues fought valiantly for the prize. I won for placing Bidex women's vaginal deodorant in a butcher shop. How did I do it? I was walking by the butcher shop one morning and noticed a long line of women waiting to pick up their orders. In a flash, I strode into the store and asked to speak to the manager. In between hacking through short loin and flank steak, he wiped his bloody hands on his apron and barked at me to come back at the end of the day. I returned at 17.30 and waited until 18.30 for him to finish serving his last customer.

"Now then lad, what do you want?" in his Yorkshire accent.

"I want to help your business."

"That's very kind of you. How are you gunna do that?"

"I want to sell you women's personal deodorant."

"Ha, are ya daft lad? Why the 'ell would I want that?" Thank goodness he didn't ask me for details as I lowered my voice at the word vaginal.

"Well, I notice you have dozens of women waiting in line to buy meat. If you use the small shelf behind you for this ladies-only product, you have the chance of increasing your sales by diversifying your product range with no extra effort on your part. Of course, this only makes sense if you agree with me that most of your customers are women."

"Go on then lad, we'll have a go, Ow much?"

I had the stock in the back of my car and sold him a carton. I even cleaned the shelf, emptied the carton and set up the display for him. I won the hundred pounds but I never dared to go back to the shop.

CHAPTER 8

The American Dream

My mother received a letter from Uncle Cyril. "I'm 64 years old, and I need Larry to come to America, to learn, and eventually take over my business." I wrote to Sandy about it, and she wrote back that she was very excited and said I should come. This timely confluence was exactly what I needed to take the plunge, even though I was still embarrassed that I didn't have a university degree. But then I realised, if I could sell vaginal deodorant to a Yorkshire butcher, how hard could New York be?

My last day of work at William Warner came, and I gave back the car, (still in good condition). On the train ride back to Leeds, I was trying to imagine what my future would hold. New York City in 1973 was filled with great social unrest, and crime rates were high. Despite this, it was the most exciting and vibrant place I imagined existed on earth. But New York was far away, and leaving my family and friends was making me homesick even before I left.

But all I had to do was imagine leaning back on the Air India flight from London to New York and imagine Sandy welcoming me at Kennedy Airport. Finally, after four years, we would actually be together in the same city. I hadn't told anyone yet, but we had even started talking about marriage.

Nine days after my 21st birthday, I had a joint birthday party with my friend Malcolm Margolis in his beautiful garden in Harrogate in North Yorkshire. We were not only celebrating our birthdays together but it was also my farewell party. Over one hundred people attended, and we had a DJ, delicious food, and an abundance of good beer and cheap wine. I danced with all my friends as the music telegraphed to all those who could hear (and the many who didn't care to hear) that I was on top of the world!

While dancing to Carly Simon's "You're So Vain", I was truly happy. "Oh my God, I'm 21 and I'm flying to New York in a few days." I was truly high and no substances beside a little wine were involved. I wouldn't have that feeling again until almost ten years later on my wedding day. As the hours drew near to leave England, the desire to see Sandy was overwhelming. Saying goodbye to my mum and Dianne was hard. It was even a little hard saying it to my dad. I could see the pride twinkling through my mother's tears as she kissed me again and again. My sister hugged me like it was the last time she would ever see me, and my father hugged me long and hard and began sobbing.

My father was now Director of Production for a company called Benjamin Simon's in Leeds which employed over 400 people in the factory. One of his major customers was Christian Dior, and he surprised me with four suits, as well as a bottle of my favourite aftershave, Aramis. He never used his connections for himself, but his factory also made the uniforms for the Air India flight crew, and he managed to get me an upgrade to a first-class seat on Air India. I'd never flown on a plane, and now I was in first class. Today I take transatlantic flights regularly and visit many countries, but that first time made me feel like a movie star.

During the last hour of the flight, I began to think about meeting

Uncle Cyril. I had corresponded with him for the past thirteen years, but due to the expense of telephone calls, I had never actually spoken with him. The plan was that I would work for and also live with him. The worry of a job and accommodation had been sorted out. Naively, of course, I never gave a minute's thought as to whether I would like to work for and indeed live with him. All I could think of was being with Sandy. As our descent into New York was announced, it was overwhelming to see the skyline from the aircraft and, at that moment, I felt like the luckiest man on the planet.

Armed with my passport and visa documents, I made my way to passport control, my heart in my mouth, as I knew I would be seeing my Sandy and, of course, Uncle Cyril standing on the other side of those sliding doors! As the customs officer looked at my passport, a frown appeared on his face, and he picked up a red phone. Immediately, two police officers arrived and asked me to follow them. Shocked and scared, I asked what it was about. They ignored me and took me to a cubicle where a custom's official wearing latex gloves told me to completely undress, while the guard remained. I asked why. Telling me to open my legs wide and bend over, he prodded me up my rectum. I screamed. He shouted, "keep still." "He's clean," he said to the guard. Welcome to America. All I wanted to do was turn around, go home, and never set foot in America again.

After I hurriedly put my clothes back on, they escorted me through the sliding doors and I saw Uncle Cyril, his girlfriend Celia, and Sandy. I was in a daze, and it was an out of body experience as I accepted their hugs of welcome. I was so traumatised that I failed to realise how strange it was that Sandy, who had come all the way to the airport to welcome me, told me I should go home with my uncle, and she would spend time with me the next evening. In a trance, I got into Cyril's waiting car and was driven to Manhattan to his apartment in the Beaux Arts building on East 44th Street. All I can remember is the blur of the traffic, skyscrapers, and the sound of the sirens. I didn't tell my uncle or Sandy about the cavity search.

The next morning, I awoke to the sound of Uncle Cyril's booming voice. My head was spinning, and I was not really sure where I was. As I peered at him through jet-lagged eyes, I saw him hit a button and the curtains flew open. I had once lived in a house with no indoor toilet, and now my curtains were controlled by a button automatically.

The first thing I asked was if Sandy had called and he said, "No, but women are like that." He helped me unpack and then suggested that I call her. "Gee, I never thought you'd have such nice clothes," he said as he saw my Dior suits. After dressing, I called Sandy, and I was so excited to hear her voice, she asked how I was. I told her I was desperate to see her. "Please, please come to the apartment now, I can't wait to see you and hold you again. I can't believe I am here and can see you when I want and not have to write those blessed letters and be satisfied with a two minute monthly phone call." I was surprised and a little taken aback that she said she had some errands to do for her mum and some school work to finish but that she would come to the apartment, and we would go for dinner at 7:00pm. I should have realised that something was strange.

The only family Uncle Cyril had was my mother, my sister, his aunt Lilly and me. Lilly still lived in Brooklyn in the same house where my mum and grandparents had lived, and she brought Cyril up when his mother passed away. Whilst my entry into the US had been traumatic, eating lunch at a deli with Cyril and walking down Fifth Avenue to his office between 38th and 39th Street on the afternoon of my first day there, I couldn't help but begin to feel excited again. The surreal trauma of the search was beginning to fade.

At the office, Cyril introduced me to all the staff, but before doing so he said, "Remember Larry who you are, please do not get too familiar with the staff. Remember you are a Marcus." This made me feel a little uncomfortable.

Sandy arrived at 7:00pm, and she looked lovely! I had expected her to jump on me and hug me like we used to do in Leeds, but she was reserved. I chalked it up to the fact that Uncle Cyril and Celia were there. After making small talk, we headed to the Top of the Sixes restaurant where Sandy had made a reservation. I felt like I was back as the star of the movie with the clinking of glasses and violins in the background. I admit that a part of me worried about the cost, but I pushed those thoughts to the side. "At the end of the day, what does it matter?" I asked myself. "I'm in a fabulous restaurant with the girl I've been waiting to be with for years and in whom I've invested so many of my dreams!"

I began to relax and leaned back in the chair as I watched her lips move as she spoke to me. I couldn't stop myself from yearning for her and a goofy smile must have sprouted on my face. But something in her tone brought me back to earth.

"...So that's why, Larry, you know I love you very, very much, and I have missed you, and I am so glad that you are in New York. I think it is a great opportunity for you, and I didn't want to do anything to stop you from coming here."

"Sandy darling, what are you talking about? You're the reason I came. Of course, there's nothing you have to worry about. Nothing would have stopped me from coming here to be with you!"

"I'm having a relationship with a guy I met at my cousin's wedding." She didn't even pause before casually saying it. "It has been going on for six months now, and I think it is only fair to share this with you as he has asked me to marry him, and I have said yes!" (I was glad to hear that they got divorced a few years later).

I had come to this golden land of opportunity filled with hope and brimming with optimism. This was supposed to be the country where my luck would change forever. Instead, I was welcomed to the New World with a finger up my bum and a dagger plunged into my heart. "Enjoy your meal, enjoy your life," stumbled out of my mouth, and I ran out of the restaurant. I don't know how I got back to Cyril's that night.

The next morning I awoke to the music of Manhattan. Sirens, car horns, and traffic like I'd never heard before. Yet the clammering outside was nothing compared to what was going on in my head. After the first few moments of morning wore off, I lay there paralysed. I managed to pull the covers up over my head as the memories rushed in. I had been on top of the world with the girl of my dreams. I had arrived and I had been dumped, unceremoniously dumped. Cyril was unceremoniously shaking my shoulder. It was time to get up.

I kicked off the blanket, ignored the electric curtains opening, and headed straight for the bathroom to take a long, hot shower. How could this dream have turned so quickly into a nightmare? Here I was, just arrived in New York, and the girl of my dreams was now marrying her teacher. I had never read about this kind of thing in books and didn't know how I was going to survive it. In the middle of my shower, there was Cyril knocking on the shower door. "C'mon Larry. Hurry up, and get ready so we can have breakfast and go!"

I jumped out of the shower and began quickly drying off. I was in the middle of pulling my trousers on when the door to the bathroom opened, and Uncle Cyril stomped back in carrying my bottle of Aramis. "Look Larry, you can't just leave a nice bottle of cologne like this lying around in the living room. Everything has its proper place, and this belongs in the bathroom. Here, put it over there." Although I was still buckling my belt, he didn't wait for me to finish before shoving the bottle in my hand and motioning to the medicine cabinet. As I leaned over to open the medicine cabinet, I dropped the bottle in the sink. To my horror, it smashed, and glass shards flew everywhere. Uncle Cyril looked me up and down and stormed out of the bathroom muttering, "Damn clumsy fool." I had left my father in England and was now living with another version in America.

I wanted to call my mum, but there was no way I dared. Phone calls were too expensive, and I didn't want Cyril even angrier with me than he already was. I zipped around the room pulling on socks, buttoning my shirt, and tucking myself in as I rushed out the door to find Cyril. Over breakfast, I told him what happened with Sandy. I had no one else to tell. He did try his best to console me and, in between bites of food, belted out, "Women ... can't live with 'em, can't live without 'em." I think he was quite touched that I had confided in him, but he kept asking for more intimate details which made me feel very uncomfortable. I had spent so many years writing to him and sharing my life in letters, that I had created this almost mythical uncle. The reality was that he bore no resemblance to that man. As he got up to leave the room, Cyril turned to me and said stoically, "It's gonna be all right. Oh by the way, please straighten your tie." Without another word, he left the room.

We arrived at the office, and Cyril said, "Larry the best way for you to learn my business is from the bottom, so today you are going to work with Cheryl in the filing room." At the end of the day, he checked my work and found a few mistakes. I was now at rock bottom.

When I got back to the apartment that night and went to my room, there was a brand new bottle of Aramis from Bloomingdales sitting on the dresser. Next to it lay a note scribbled in Cyril's handwriting, "For my dear nephew, Larry." This was not a comfort, this was another version of my dad, who would beat me up and then want to hug and kiss me. I climbed into bed and sobbed.

Look where I am now, I have given up my life in England, my friends, my family, I have been violated by the customs, dumped by my girlfriend and reduced to a filing clerk, and not even a good one.

Should I go home? Should I stick it out with Cyril?

CHAPTER 9

Uncle Cyril

As the days rolled by, I began discovering new quirks about Cyril. I considered myself a tidy person, but he crossed over the border to OCD land. Every morning, he would enter my room, uninvited, and check to make sure the bed was made, and everything was in order. I'd then stand before him as he inspected what I was wearing.

The first time I wore one of the Christian Dior suits my father had made for me, he looked me up and down, and then said, "Nice suit. But your shoes are dirty. Go clean them." I took off my shoes and began to wipe them clean with a cloth. If my father had said anything like this, even with the threat of being hit, I wouldn't have held back. I would have told him where to stick his brush. I felt beaten up emotionally, which was far worse than any physical violence I had experienced from my father.

The nit-picking about my clothing was only the beginning. He loved chess and most nights I had to spend an hour playing with him. But he'd usually beat me in three moves, and then shake his head. He so wanted me to be good, but he only made me feel like a failure. Next, he took me to play golf with him, and I couldn't hit any of the balls. He had me demoted to the golf buggy driver, which I almost overturned every time I carted him around. Yet again, he looked me up and down and shook his head in disappointment.

Cyril had been a music major at Columbia University and loved classical music. I had been sacked from the school choir for not being able to hit a note. But that didn't stop him from playing a game with me whenever he had the chance. He'd play a segment of some of his favourite classical music pieces on the record player, lift the needle, and test me. "Who is the composer? What is the name of the piece?" For every answer I got right, I'd get a point. I usually got a grand score of one. He soon realised the only pieces I knew were Beethoven's "duh duh duh duh" Symphony No. 5 in C Minor and Tchaikovsky's 1812 Overture, and that was only thanks to the cannons. He'd always play one of these songs so at least I'd walk away with one point.

One of his most frustrating habits that I had to endure was when he would take Celia and me out to a restaurant. After we were seated, he'd always say,

"OK, Larry, what would you like?"

"Well, I'm really not in the mood tonight for meat so maybe I'll try ..."

"No, no Larry," he'd interrupt. "You must try the steak. It is absolutely delicious."

"Thank you Uncle Cyril. It's OK, I think I'll go for the pasta with the ..."

"OK waiter, we'll have three steaks, medium rare!"

I couldn't even order my own damn food. I had lived away from my parents for the past few years, and now I had this guy who meant well, but was inadvertently chipping away at my self-esteem. When I was around him, I felt like a failure at everything - chess, music, my clothing and even my taste in food. Even more demeaning were the jobs he had me do at his company.

After a while, I realised that he wouldn't have thought that someone my age would have had the work experience I did. How could he? I had been too embarrassed to say that I'd left school at 15. I needed to tell him what I had done and what I was capable of. So I sat down with Cyril and Celia and told him all the things I had accomplished back in England. They sat there in silence and then he asked Celia to leave the room. "Larry, I'm embarrassed that you showed off. You made yourself look like a fool in front of Celia. You need to be more humble." I was humbled, humiliated, and embarrassed about what I had said and went for a long walk in Central Park. I even asked the ducks in The Pond, "Had I showed off? Should I be ashamed of myself? Should I die of embarrassment?" The answer was no.

Yet, just like my father, he was complicated. On Sundays, he would buy the New York Times and would give me articles to read, and then we'd discuss them, which made me feel like his equal. One Sunday, we were reading about an Alaskan pipeline he was thinking of investing in, and he asked for my thoughts. Later that week, he bought 75,000 shares in my name which in UK cash terms meant I could have bought a three bedroom flat. I thought to myself that maybe he really does take me seriously.

I was overwhelmed by Cyril's generosity when he bought me a Mustang car for my birthday. I was thrilled and terrified, driving in Manhattan was traumatic. I had no sense of direction and I would always get lost. On more than one occasion, I would pull over the car, get out and hail a taxi, I'd tell the driver where I needed to go and would pay him to lead the way, and I would follow in convoy.

When I returned from The Pond in Central Park, Cyril asked me in a solemn tone to come and sit by his desk as he wanted to talk further with me. I was nervous, sick to my stomach. I sat, held my breath, and waited for bad news. He opened the top drawer of his desk and passed me a document. I opened it and, as I did, he told me that I was going to be the main beneficiary of his will. I couldn't believe my ears. He was a multi-millionaire. This was a pattern, first of all kick me and take me down followed by an act of great generosity although I had to admit, it did initially work.

For the next few days, I felt like I was walking on air. I had won the lottery. But in a very short time that winning lottery ticket trapped me in a golden cage. He was in his late 60s and, at 21, I thought I was going to inherit a fortune in the foreseeable future. I gritted my teeth and focused on my future inheritance and tried to ignore how miserable I was working for him. Leaving seemed impossible; there was too much at stake for my family and me. Like many other people who had a prospective inheritance, I was trapped.

I wrote letters home regularly. Putting it down on paper had a cathartic effect, and I was able to keep going. Initially, my family were very excited at the news regarding the will. It would be life changing for our family. I also began to share with my mother and father how difficult Cyril was and eventually how unhappy I was feeling.

My social life was the one thing that had improved. I made a few new friends and spending time with them was an escape from the demands of Uncle Cyril. It was one of these friends who eventually helped me escape.

Howie was a close friend of one of my friends back in Leeds, and we had become fairly close since I moved to the US. It was great to have an American friend who was exceptionally kind and caring. He taught at the Perkins Institute in Boston and came into New York occasionally and introduced me to some of his friends in the city. But whenever I could, I'd take a Greyhound bus to visit him in Boston. Of course, Cyril wasn't fond of these trips, asking questions like, "Do they do drugs?" But I loved freeing myself from my midtown cage and visiting

Howie and his friends. I met Naomi, the best friend of Howie's current girlfriend, who worked in a venereal disease clinic in Boston. She was pretty, with big, sparkling blue eyes, and a sunshine personality. We all had a lot of fun together.

Cyril was right though. Every time I got out of the lift, I was greeted by Howie and Naomi, loud music, and the strong smell of marijuana. As a teen, I was always comfortable to flirt but would rarely take it further. That changed after Sandy. There I was in Howie's apartment, listening to Led Zeppelin's Stairway to Heaven with a glass of cheap wine, and taking my first drag on a joint. Many people have told me that they felt nothing when they first tried weed. Not in my case. Maybe because I was so stressed, I got this most wonderful feeling of happiness. Inhaling was not a problem as I was a heavy smoker at the time. Kathy, the gin girl at Debenhams, taught me how to smoke. I found myself diving into Naomi's blue eyes, giving me a release I hadn't felt for a long time. I even forgot that Naomi worked in a VD clinic.

The next day, Howie took me to see where he worked. It was an institute for the blind and deaf. One of the programmes they offered was teaching deaf children how to dance. They had a studio outfitted with large speakers that created vibrations on the floor. The instructors would encourage the students to feel the vibrations and then move to the beat. It was thrilling to see these deaf children react to the musical vibrations. When I was a kid, I wasn't good at rugby, but I loved to dance. My sister used to take classes at Madame Carr's Ballet School in the basement of the Clock Cinema when she was eight and I was six. I'd sit with my Mum and watch Dianne dance as I swayed my legs back and forth to the music. One of the teachers said to my mother, "Let Laurence join in." But in those days, boys didn't do ballet, unless you were Russian. But from the moment I began dancing ballet, I took to it like a duck to water. I was more excited about it than my sister who was not a particularly elegant dancer. This created arguments between my parents as my mother was happy I enjoyed it so much, and my father was terrified that this was a sign I was going to "become a poof". When he couldn't convince my mother to forbid ballet, he just increased the number of rugby games he dragged me to. I still like to dance.

Howie saw how excited I was about the dance studio and offered me a job on the spot. I think he knew I felt like a failure in New York. I accepted it right then and there without even thinking for one moment about my job, Uncle Cyril, the will, and my family. I began working with the deaf kids the next day. For the first time, I was not in a commercial environment and felt fulfilled and needed. It ended up that the institute couldn't offer me a salary because my visa was connected to Cyril's business, so I only stayed for two weeks.

When I returned to New York, the will that had been locked away was now placed in the drawer of the writing desk that we both used. I couldn't resist reading it. It became a daily reminder of what I would lose if I were to leave. Cyril arranged for me to meet with his lawyer to discuss the will. But I had tasted a moment of happiness, and my confidence in myself had returned. So when Howie told me that he was taking a road trip up to Montreal, I didn't hesitate to tell Cyril I was travelling again. He asked me when I would come back. The plan was that we would spend a weekend in Montreal, but I told him I'd call to let him know.

I had never been to Canada and was excited for the trip. Although I had very little money in my pocket, I was going to be spending the weekend with Howie, his girlfriend, and Naomi. This would be the first time Naomi and I would get to spend an entire weekend together, and I was looking forward to it. When we got to Montreal, we had a barbeque under a star-lit night. In those days, people in the UK didn't have barbeques; we just watched Americans have them on TV. So as I munched on my hot dog and gazed up at the moon, I felt free.

The relationship with Naomi didn't work out. I can't even remember why. I think it might have been the lack of marijuana or my fear of catching VD from her. I was scared she could have caught it from one of her patients and then given it to me. I was a complete ignoramus of how STDs were transmitted and had been checking myself every time we had sex to be sure my willy hadn't dropped off!

Old Montreal was beautiful, and I was especially impressed with the romantic cobblestone alleys. The architecture was magnificent. Whilst I was in a coffee shop, the guy behind the counter saw my B'nai B'rith pin, which I always wore on my jacket lapel, and excitedly asked if I was a member.

"Yes, I was actually a president of my junior chapter back in England."

"Wow, that's so cool, man. What are you doing here in Montreal?"

"Just visiting. But I wish I could stay here."

"Well, guess what, man? I'm a member of B'nai B'rith, and I'd be happy to host you at my place if you want to stay."

"What? Are you kidding me?"

But he wasn't kidding, and he even offered me a job working in the coffee shop. So I said goodbye to Howie, who was happy for me, and grabbed my bag from his car. When I had arrived in the US, I had four fancy Christian Dior suits and a large suitcase stuffed with clothes. Now, I had a small duffle bag with some jeans, a couple of T-shirts, a razor, and not much money.

After a week of serving people coffee and wiping up spills and messes around the shop, I called my mum just to tell her where I was. I made a reverse charge call as I didn't have the money to afford it myself. "I'm furious. How could you not call us or your Uncle Cyril?" She said that Cyril had been contacting her, frantically wanting to know where I was, and was wanting to welcome me back to the business.

At this moment, I did feel bad, and my honest reaction to hearing that Cyril wanted me back was relief. I had quickly come to the realisation I wasn't cut out to work in a coffee shop and allowed myself to accept that it wasn't for me. So I called my Uncle Cyril who said he was sorry that it hadn't worked out. "I love you. Please come home." I was touched and relieved. Wishing my new Canadian friend *au revoir*, I returned to New York.

I had changed countries and employment, but when I got back, Cyril hadn't changed a bit. As soon as he opened the door and saw me in my scruffy jeans with a duffle bag slung over my shoulder, he greeted me with, "Have you had a shower?" I had expected a hug. I blushed, muttered something, and went to my room to unpack. I had just finished taking a shower when Cyril's voice boomed, "Larry, you have a phone call!"

I rolled my eyes. It was probably Howie calling to make sure I wasn't dead. I calmly dried off my hair with a soft towel and reached for my pants on the bed. "It's from England!" I was out in seconds, pressing the phone hard to my cheek.

"No, nothing bad has happened," my sister said.

"Everyone is OK. I have good news to tell you Larry. I'm pregnant."

Something broke inside me. In an instant, I didn't care about my American dream anymore. I just wanted to go home.

I listened as Dianne told me all about it, then my mum got on the phone, and I fought back my sobs. Cyril and Celia left the apartment. As he closed the door, Cyril motioned to me and, for the first time since I had arrived, actually whispered, "Take all the time you want Larry."

After talking with my mum for a few minutes about Canada, Howie, and what life was like in America she suddenly said, "There's someone here who wants to talk with you. He's been hovering all over me."

"How are you doing, son?"

"All right, Dad."

"Really?"

"Yeah, I just miss Dianne and Mum."

"Humph. How's it working out with Cyril?"

"I ... I hate it. I hate working for him."

"Humph. Well, why don't you just come back home then?"

"I can't do that. He'd cut me out of the will, and then we'd lose all that money."

"He said that?"

"No, but why wouldn't he?"

There was a long pause. "To hell with the will, Larry. If you don't like it there, you tell Cyril that you want to come home."

"But the money, Dad," letting that sentence float between us for a few seconds.

"Screw the damn money. If you want to leave, then come back home."

Again, my Dad said something that changed my life.

That night, I couldn't sleep as I was psyching myself up for a difficult conversation with him. The next day I waited until we got to the office to tell him that I was leaving and returning to the UK. His face remained expressionless. I had collected all the papers his lawyer made me sign and told him that I wanted to go home. He shrugged.

I handed back the paperwork for the 75,000 Alaskan pipeline shares and the keys to the car. Taking a deep breath, I told him I came to America with $300 and had $50 left. I would appreciate it if he would give me $250. Without saying a word, he took $250 in crisp bills, and I stood up to shake his hand. He shook my hand, but didn't say a word.

I said "Goodbye and thank you for everything," and I was out of there without a thought.

I felt proud and liberated, but didn't give a second thought about how Cyril was feeling, and what I was leaving behind. I was going home. I left his apartment, headed for Kennedy airport without a ticket, but as luck would have it, I arrived 3 hours before a British Airways flight back to England. This time, I had to pay for economy which cost $85 which reduced my total wealth to $215, what a result!

CHAPTER 10

Exodus from America

Dreams, shattered. Those were the words I kept thinking about after I told Cyril I wanted nothing to do with his will and was making my exodus from America. Those first few hours had been euphoric and liberating. But as I sat on the plane back to England, I knew I would soon be in the place where I had started, with no money, no job, and no direction. Then it dawned on me, it was going to get worse. I was going to have to move back in with my parents, with whom I had not lived for more than four years. When I reflected on the arguments with my father, the realisation of what I had done began to sink in.

Trees whizzed by the train window, and I started to recognise the landmarks near Leeds, I realised I couldn't wait to see my family, old friends, and even my dad, I was so happy to be back. Thank God I couldn't open the doors before the train stopped; otherwise I would have jumped out onto the tracks. As the train came into the station, there on the platform was my sister, my pregnant sister. I rushed off the train and I enveloped her with a big hug. She didn't hug back, but that was ok. She wasn't much of a hugger anyway, and then my dad embraced me and wouldn't let go, telling me how thrilled he was that I was home again. I wondered how long it would last. Mum, who was in a wheelchair at this point, was waiting at home. After all the hugging, all I wanted to do was see my mum.

I was surprised about how small Leeds seemed compared to how I remembered it. Even though I had only spent a few months in America, I definitely experienced not just the physical size of the country but a whole new culture and political environment which continued to shape my ideas about the world.

It was brilliant to see my mum again. I cried and peppered her with hugs and kisses.

"Enough, enough, Larry". But she didn't put up her hands to stop me so I knew she was just as excited to see me again.

"Don't think you're staying under this roof for free, now. You need to contribute some money!" I had been viewing my homecoming through rose-tinted glasses, and I fought back the feelings that I may have made a huge mistake. "Well, I would be getting a fortune of money if you hadn't encouraged me to leave Uncle Cyril," was what I wanted to shout at him, but I bit my tongue. I knew that his permission to give up the will was exactly what I had needed at the time. But that still didn't stop me from being angry. He was the one who had encouraged me to let go of Uncle Cyril's inheritance, and now he wanted rent money. I had been home for three hours.

I think he was disappointed that I hadn't brought home the golden treasure. To my family, working with Cyril was the opportunity of a lifetime, any sympathy I had earned had disappeared, just like their inheritance.

As I sat on my bed in my old room, it hit me. "You're not here on holiday. You've come back. The last time you were here, you had a grand farewell party and embarked on a journey to chase your golden future with Uncle Cyril and, of course, with Sandy. But that's all over now."

As I laid down on my bed looking up at the ceiling, I noticed the curtains were definitely not electronic like in Cyril's Manhattan apartment. "This isn't the beginning of an adventure. It's the end of one."

As I rolled over, I tried to convince myself I wasn't a failure. But, to be honest, that is how I was beginning to feel. In addition to that, the daily letters and monthly telephone calls with my girlfriend Sandy had been an important part of my life and, at that moment, I felt more bereft about our relationship than I had allowed myself to feel during my time in New York. My future looked bleak.

Andy White was the first friend to come see me. A few years later, he would encourage me to start my first business. Once again, I had no car, and my father refused to lend me his. "Great, another reminder of what I don't have." There was only one bus every hour to the city centre and Leeds had no underground. I just wanted Andy to pick me up and get me out of the house.

We went to the local pub and seeing many close friends, including Michael Caplin, cheered me up. I hadn't expected it, but my time in America made me something of a celebrity among my friends.

"What does America really look like?"

"Does New York smell as bad as London?"

"Did Sandy really dump you for another bloke?"

At one point, Andy was telling me how now he had graduated from university, he was living in London, and working for a company that sold camping equipment. As he said that, the thought struck me. "London. That's where I've got to go. If I stay in Leeds, I'll keep comparing it to New York. London is also a city shimmering with bright lights!" As if he could read my mind, Michael Caplin took a swig of his beer, wiped his mouth, and said, "You know what? You should come to London with me. You can stay at my flat until you find a job and get your own place. It'll be great!"

The next week, I was on a train to London. Big Ben, a hardwood floor, and a sleeping bag greeted me.

Michael was such a good friend, but he did not have Aramis aftershave waiting for me. Usually, there wasn't even toilet paper waiting for me. Every time I looked at the windows, I thought of electric curtains. To this day, I have two absolute requirements for my houses: electronic curtains and luxurious bathrooms.

Now that I was in London, I had to start earning money. I had a lot of experience for a guy who was 22, but what skills did I have that would land me a job quickly? It turned out to be shorthand and typing.

I made an appointment at a nearby employment agency. My end goal was to leverage my experiences and accomplishments into a great job in sales (which offered a car) or in retail (which offered more money). But, first I had to get any job I could for one very strategic reason: I needed to eat and contribute towards the rent. The $215 I returned to England with was quickly disappearing before my eyes, and I didn't want to sponge off Michael more than I already was. Once I had a job, any job, I could begin hunting for a better job.

As I sat down for my appointment at the Reliance Employment agency and told them my skill set, Samantha, the girl interviewing me raised her eyebrows. "You do shorthand and typing? Did I hear that correctly?" She wasn't about to let some provincial from Leeds pull the wool over her eyes. So she tested me on the spot. As my fingers flew across the typewriter for the speed test, I heard her giggle in astonishment. I didn't do so well taking dictation, but I did pass the test. If she had been older, I would have been pissed off. But she was young and pretty and hearing her giggle made me feel good. She told me she could get me a temp job at Royds Advertising in the West End, working for 63 pence an hour. "Great, I can get instant money!" I thanked her, shook her hand, and walked away with a job for the next morning (and her number).

I stayed up the whole night before my first assignment, reviewing my shorthand. I knew it would be odd that a man was coming in for a job as a secretary so I wanted to get my skills up to speed. When I arrived for work the next morning, the manager had a fit. "I don't want a clerk who is a guy! I want a secretary! Tell your incompetent agency that I want a damn secretary, not a male clerk!"

I knew exactly what I had to do next. I didn't yell back at him, although the testosterone coursing through my veins was telling me to do exactly that. Instead, I folded my legs over and looked him straight in the eye and said, "Excuse me Mr. Davis, I AM a secretary!" I then batted my eyes and stared at him. He looked nervous and more than a little uncomfortable.

He motioned his hand and some grumpy lady walked over and took me down the hall to an office with glass walls and a manual typewriter in the centre of a desk. She sat me there and said, "Stay here until they call you for dictation." After 30 minutes, no one had called for me. So I got up, went to Mr. Davis and told him I am getting paid 63 pence an hour and that I didn't want to get paid for doing nothing. "Fine, you want to be a secretary. Sit down, and let's see if you can take down my dictation."

I grabbed a pencil and sat down with my legs crossed resting my shorthand pad on my knee and when he was finished dictating, I returned to my all-glass office and began furiously typing it up. At some point, I felt the hairs on the back of my neck stand up. I looked up, and there were five people staring at me through the glass window as if I were a circus act. This was not the first time I was being stereotyped for being a male secretary, but this time I was getting paid.

Luckily, it was only a temp job, and I was out of there a week later.

Samantha called to tell me she had a potential permanent job for me working for a large medical insurance provider called BUPA. We went out for drinks to discuss the job. (But I knew she wanted more, which helped me restore my battered ego!). The new job was an internal auditing job where I'd be sent to Oxford for a six-week training course, all expenses paid, and that was the main attraction. At least I could eat, and I wouldn't be a temp secretary forever. The requirement for the job was a university degree. Thanks to Samantha, I used poetic licence and indicated that I had failed my degree because in my final year I had been involved in family issues and had mitigating circumstances. She said that would gain me some sympathy, and it definitely worked. To be perfectly honest, it was rather more than a little poetic licence.

To my complete surprise, I got the job at BUPA and was sent to Oxford for the training. The high school dropout was now an enrolled student at Oxford! My mum was so proud (even though it was at the BUPA office and not the university, but that's just a small detail). When asked where I was, Mum would delight in telling people I was "at Oxford".

I learned all about adding clauses to patients' health insurance coverage which would exclude their previous conditions which is normal in the insurance business. I also learned more about medical terminology than any non-doctor ever needs to know. I had to observe medical procedures like mastectomies, lumpectomies, bilateral varicose veins, and hip replacements as they were some of the most popular insurance claims, and BUPA wanted me to be knowledgeable enough to make informed decisions.

BUPA was an ethical company and, if there was money left over, they would pay out extra money to ease the pain for their patients. I actually had the power to accept or reject claims and, whilst I did take advice from colleagues, I rarely rejected claims. After my first year, I had the feeling that this career was not for me.

My previous jobs had all pretty much been in retail where I met customers like those you see in Walmart – generally, housewives and young families. But BUPA was a widely respected non-profit in the healthcare sector and attracted a wide array of aristocrats and the British posh in its network of board and benefactors. This was a completely different environment than any I had worked in before. Now I had to attend fundraising dinners, look smart, and act in that formal and charming way that the British upper class expected. My manager even made me use my full name.

"Larry just sounds too much like an American cowboy. We prefer you to use Laurence which is much more respectable." I was tempted to tell him this wasn't the first time my name had been changed, but held back. I had to adapt to their style of conversation and blend in. I learned that I didn't have to change myself, rather I had to adapt myself. I needed to listen very hard to what they were saying, how they say it, and then test it out in conversation. I watched their facial expressions, mirrored, and echoed how they spoke, and learned how to place my hand in my pockets the same way that they did. If they used certain phrases, I took a mental note and repeated it later in conversation. I had learned these skills back in my sales training sessions at William Warner's, and I used it now, not to sell products, but to sell myself. They call this technique mirroring.

Another tip was to ask open-ended questions. You should never ask a question that doesn't start with the words "why, what, when, who, or how." Ask them, "What did you think of the lecture?" it is then impossible to give a yes or no answer. I often use it today to understand what someone is thinking or feeling.

One afternoon, Samantha called me. She asked me if I'd meet

her for a drink after work. As we sat down at the bar, she said "I have a proposition for you!" I said, "Oh great, I've been waiting for a proposition from you for a while." She laughed and said she had something else in mind. She told me her company had a vacancy for a trainee recruiter for their temporary employment division. She told me all about the details of the job as I looked intently into her eyes.

As we sipped our drinks, she smiled and said, "I think you'd be great at it. With your varied experience, you understand the world of work better than a lot of people our age. Plus, I think you're cute." After that evening, we became more than business associates for a short time.

I loved my new job as a recruiter at Reliance. Since the majority of the work was over the phone, the trainer taught us telephone selling and interviewing techniques. Another part of the job was preparing candidates for their job interviews, something with which I had a lot of experience!

The trainer also constantly reminded us that we were detectives and our job was to find out the truth about people. Modelling ourselves after the police was fun, but one police technique that was often used in interrogation changed my life: The power of silence.

I had to consciously remember the technique as being silent was and still is not one of my natural skills. Most people are uncomfortable with silence. That is exactly what I was taught to look for, those moments when silence could motivate people to share valuable information about themselves. If you ask someone why they left their last job, they may respond quickly with something short and prepared like, "I was bored, and the money was poor." The key is to control yourself from responding and just wait. After a few agonising moments, they are likely to get so uncomfortable with the silence that they will say something that actually informs you more about their last job. If you can restrain yourself, they'll probably tell you much more than they ever intended.

This technique works on everyone. Even sullen teenagers can succumb to this technique. I know this because I've used it on my own. My kids tell me they prefer me to shout at them rather than ask questions and leave long silences.

I loved implementing my new training on sales calls and interviews, but I had one major problem. God gifted me with an unusually high-pitched voice. People have often thought, especially on the telephone, that I was a woman, or face-to-face that I was gay because it was just that high a pitch.

I was making a call to an American oil company based in London who I knew had more potential job openings than any other company in Central London. As the man on the other line picked up, I enthusiastically said, "Hello Tom, my name is Laurence, and I'm from Reliance Employment. I want to find out what your present staff situation is, and how we can help you?" You know how you can hear someone smile on a phone call? He said, "Well, Florence. What ways can you help me?"

I knew that people responded differently to a pretty girl than to your average Joe, and now it was happening to me. He obviously misheard me and thought I was named Florence, and he was flirting with me! I was too embarrassed to correct him, so I cleared my throat and in my coolest falsetto responded, "Well Sir, I can help you in a temporary way or a permanent way. That is, if you'll let me."

Six weeks later, I had over 20 people working at his office and had become a hero in my office. Tom kept finding excuses to call me, and it kept getting harder and harder to find the nerve to keep up the pretence as the flirting became more overt. Eventually, I let myself realise the power of flirtatious conversation. Everything was going well until the day he called to tell me he was coming to London to visit.

"Hi Florence, how are you my dear?"

"I'm doing great. How are you?"

"I'm coming into London to visit and would love to meet you in person."

"Oh wow. That sounds lovely."

"Ha, ha. Great because I think it's about time you took me out to lunch."

"Oh lovely, what's the best time for you?"

"Next Monday at 1:15pm. I'll get you the details."

"Great, Tom. I'm really looking forward to it."

I put down the phone and immediately went into a total panic, "F*ck, f*ck, f*ck!" After sitting at my desk and pulling my hair out trying to come up with a solution, I got up and made a beeline for my manager's office. "Excuse me sir, I'm in a very difficult position and need to talk to you."

He sat me down and listened to the whole story. I was hoping he'd be sympathetic, but he just gave me this strange smile and said, "OK FLORRY, you're going to have to leave Central London. They're one of our fastest growing clients, thanks to you. We'll make sure to find another branch for you to work from. As for Tom, we'll just tell him that you had a family emergency and needed to leave town."

I was loving the drama of working in Central London which, although cool and exciting, it was also a troubled time with various IRA bomb attacks on the city. So there was some relief moving out of the centre as I had been freaked out when four weeks prior to my move, I had posted over 100 envelopes in the post box at the end of the arcade where I worked. One hour later, the post box exploded from a letter bomb sent by the IRA.

"But I love working in Central London!" He gave me that strange smile again. "Well, come back with a deeper voice then." When I told Andy who was my new flatmate, he thought it was hilarious and pretty soon he had me laughing too. I was annoyed that I had to move to another branch and made sure I left a note. "Dear Tom, so sorry I can't make it. Due to family circumstances, I had to return to Yorkshire. You've been great to work with, and I'm sure my manager will take care of you." I never spoke to Tom again, but a week later he sent the London branch a huge box of chocolates with instructions to forward to me. His note read; "For the lady with the beautiful voice. Wishing you much success, and I hope we will meet someday."

After the "Florence" episode, my company moved me to the branch in Edgware, a suburb of London, a long way out of Central London. I still didn't have a car so I had to take public transport, adding insult to injury.

Michael moved back to Leeds for a new job and Andy followed to work in his father's jewellery business. He was a wonderful flatmate and friend who had helped me through difficult times. He was more like a brother, and I was sorry to see him go. So I started my search for a new place to live by looking in the shared flat page in the newspapers, as I certainly couldn't afford a flat on my own. It was both a fun and miserable experience as I viewed a number of flats, each time interviewed by prospective flatmates so that both parties could decide if they wanted to share their home after a 60-minute interview.

I arrived at Alvanley Gardens, an impressive looking house in West Hampstead, which was a great area. Normally, adverts state whether they wanted a male or female to share but the advert for Alvanley Gardens didn't specify. I was most surprised to note that the occupants were all girls, and they were looking for a fourth person to replace the person who had left to get married. Hilary was an opera singer, Elaine was a primary school teacher, and Irene worked in the accounts department of a garage.

After a gruelling interview, I was somewhat surprised as the norm was to say that they would call and let me know if they were going to offer me a place. Instead, they asked me to leave the room and wait in the hallway, I was just about to leave after waiting for more than 10 minutes as I heard the murmured voices discussing my suitability. I really wanted to be chosen for two reasons – the flat was really comfortable and the rent was affordable. Also there was a new sitcom on TV called Robin's Nest and in this programme Robin shared with three girls, and he looked to be having a great time.

I didn't have a great time, it was actually quite a nightmare. I can also agree with an article that I read that stated when women live together, they tend to have their periods at the same time, so at least one week every month was a nightmare in my flat. The yelling, the crying, the late night girl talks.

The great thing was that when one of the girls left, she was replaced by an Australian accountant called Suzanne from Melbourne. In a very short space of time, I fell in love with this very sweet and intense vegetarian. There was the extra pressure of living as a couple with two other housemates, and she felt that she needed her own place. She found it especially hard when Hillary would practice her scales at 7.30am followed by several minutes of gargling in the one and only bathroom. Every evening we were treated to the singing of Arias, this is probably why I hate the opera. After a tumultuous relationship, we decided it would be best to split up. Our split was very painful and tearful; however, within three weeks we had made up and were back together. Although I kept my room at the flat and used it as an office, I spent most of my time at Suzanne's.

Once again, it was my father who swooped in and saved the day. He called me from Leeds and told me he knew of a company looking for a sales rep in London and the South of England, and he had already suggested they hire me. "They pay well, plus they have something else you'll like". "What's that, Dad?" "They have a company car." I kissed the receiver of the phone.

I got the job, and my father was thrilled. From the way he told everyone about it, I wasn't sure what made him happier, the fact that I was a good candidate or that he had done something that had dramatically changed my life. Either way, he deserved the credit.

I still laugh when I think about how a large part of my career path in my early years was based simply off which company would give me a car.

I'll never forget the day my new company car was delivered. A four-door 1975 Hillman Hunter with a shiny metallic turquoise finish. Through the reflection of my giddy face on the glass window, I could see the black leather interior and the radio that came with a cassette player in the dashboard. I couldn't believe my luck. I opened the door and let the smell of brand new car leather wash over me. I melted into the embrace of the seat and locked the doors. I let my fingers grip the steering wheel, I put the radio on, I did a dance in my seat and sang along to Carole King's, "You've Got a Friend." **Yes! Yes! Yes!**

I leaned my head back against the headrest and smiled. I hadn't felt this good since the plane left America for England. Three days later, I crashed the Hillman.

CHAPTER 11

A Promotion

My new job was as technical sales manager for AMF Clarbro in the apparel division selling textile machines. AMF was one of the top 100 US companies in the world. Within the first two months, I had crashed the Hillman three times. Luckily, they never fired me. I attribute this to the fact that I didn't tell them. Instead, I stashed the car on a quiet block near my flat and dusted off my telesales skills from so long ago to help me sell without a car. While I had just been working at Reliance Employment two months prior, I had now moved out of the flat in Alvanley Gardens into my own flat in Kentish Town and I had my own car, so those days felt like ages ago. To meet my monthly sales quota, I started calling up my customers and selling to them on the fact that I couldn't make the trip to see them.

"I can't get to you in person for the next couple of weeks, but I will stay on the phone as long as you need so I can deal with all of your requirements …"

It turned out that most people were fine with a phone call and for those customers who I needed to see in person, I hopped on a bus or train. Turns out that because I wasn't wasting time travelling back and forth between customers, I began trebling my monthly sales quota, and,

Larry J Gould

after twelve months, I was top salesman, beating my five colleagues who had been in their jobs for a number of years.

But in the back of my mind was the fear that it would go all to pot if they ever found out I wasn't using the company car. So I got a friend who knew about these things and he tinkered with the milometer and made it look like I was putting many more miles on the Hillman. I convinced myself doing this was OK because I matched up the milometer logs with the travel expenses for the public transportation I sometimes had to take. But nothing lasts forever and one day, my boss called me at home. I was in a total panic and convinced I would be fired presently.

"Larry", he said, (I was back to being called Larry) "We've discovered some anomalies in your submissions for travel expenses."

I gulped. "Um, what do you mean?"

"Our auditor was reviewing your expense reports, and the maths just doesn't add up. For the amount of area you're covering and the customers you're seeing, plus the current cost of petrol, you should be racking up a much larger expenses claim. Yet, the amount of reimbursements you've been requesting are unusually low for the amount of sales visits you are making."

He went on to say, "Larry this is the first time I have to question somebody's expenses for being too low. Larry what is your explanation?"

I could barely speak. This was it, my moment of truth. Images of me being sacked flashed through my mind as a bead of sweat trickled down the back of my neck. Except that time-honoured excuse saying that my dog ate my car or I had developed the superpower of flight, I couldn't think of anything to say. So, out of the sheer lack of options, I just told him the truth.

My knuckles turned white as I gripped the telephone. There was a long pause. I prepared myself for the worst and was nearly passing out when I heard a strange sound on the line. Was he choking with shock? Oh my God, he was cracking up.

"Well Larry, that was quite creative of you. Truth be told, you should not have kept all that a secret but, instead of trying to skive off work, you really rose to the occasion. I'm actually impressed. Keep up the good work and my advice to you is to increase your expenses, and I have some good news for you."

I was dumbfounded. Had telling the truth actually worked? He seemed to sense my shock and kept laughing.

"Larry, since you have trouble getting around in cars, I'm going to assign you to the export sales department where you'll join the international sales team. They don't drive, they fly."

"Wait, isn't that a promotion?"

"Why, yes it is."

I wasn't fired, I was promoted.

I learned two lessons from this experience. Firstly, trickery might have saved me in the short term, but honesty rewarded me for the long term. It reinforced what my Mum had taught me when she scolded me for using my Yorkshire Penny Bank money to buy ice cream. Secondly, I learned that by capitalising on alternative forms of communication like the telephone, I was able to dramatically increase my results. It's true that sometimes you have to meet someone in person, but often a phone call works just as well. I learned to work smarter, not just harder.

AMF Clarbro was one of the top 100 US companies with its British headquarters in Leeds. Despite being thrilled at this dream job offer, I had this sinking feeling. Even with the travel, I would have to move back home. I was happy in London. Things were really working out with my Suzanne and the thought of that relationship ending was unbearable. As I drove back to London, I realised it was commitment time. If I was going to ask Suzanne to come back to Leeds with me, it would be a huge change for her as she loved her job. I knew it would be make or break, and in the back of my mind I knew I could not refuse this job. The move to Leeds prompted a serious conversation about our future lives together, and I was so excited when she said she would be happy to come to Leeds to live with me and if things worked out, we would get married. I was high! Five days before I was due to leave London for Leeds, I went back to my flat to pack up and sleep there for the next couple of nights. I was on top of the world. I had a new job and Suzanne was coming with me.

At 7:30am my phone rang waking me up. It was Suzanne. She was sobbing, and sounded heartbroken. I couldn't get her to tell me what the problem was, but told her I would come to see her immediately. I was sure something really terrible had happened. Perhaps a parent had passed away. When she answered the door, she looked terrible, and hung onto me saying, "I'm sorry, I'm sorry." She told me a guy who we had both met recently at a friend's dinner party had called her the day before, and he had stayed the night. My body turned to cold stone, and I simply said, "If you really care for me and love me as you say, please, never ever call me again." With that I left and drove back to my flat very calmly. When I got to my flat, I simply sobbed.

I returned to Leeds, maxed out my credit cards and borrowed money from my Nana Gould which I needed to put down a deposit to buy my own flat. I was shocked when I jokingly broached the idea, and Nana immediately offered to help. This was amazing because my sister was always her favourite. As she gave me the cheque, she pointed her index finger and sternly said "Don't tell Dianne".

After being back in Leeds for only two weeks, still living with my parents, I returned home one evening and my mother told me that Suzanne had called and asked me to call her back. I told my mum I had no intention of calling. Two days later, I received a letter from her, telling me she had married Robert! On the same day that I received a letter from my lawyer telling me that I had completed on a flat next to Roundhay Park.

I managed to complete the deal, days before my 25th birthday. I was a home owner. But I was empty. That feeling lasted quite a long time, except for the passion I had for my work.

CHAPTER 12

On the Road Again

My first trip as part of the export team was to attend a trade show in Bucharest, Romania selling automated textile machinery. I was delighted about my promotion, and the fact that I'd never have to worry about crashing the Hillman again and it was only when the plane began its descent that I began thinking about the last time I had landed in a new country. I immediately began to bite my nails. I vividly remembered the strip search at Kennedy Airport. As I walked off the plane, I was being probed by the eyes of dozens of Soviet security guards brandishing machine guns. I was almost paralysed with fear.

But I had no need to worry. I breezed through customs and then was whisked off in a taxi to the most luxurious hotel in the city. As I checked into my room, the red light on the phone blinked. I picked it up and, through the crackles, heard a frantic message from my Managing Director back in Leeds. My boss had fallen ill and couldn't make it. Paul Brooke, my Managing Director told me, even though this was my first assignment, I'd have to take the lead. After hanging up the phone, I began hyperventilating and lectured myself.

"Larry, they just promoted you. You can't afford to mess this up. If this goes wrong, after what you did with the Hillman, they'll sack you for sure. Hold it. Hold it. Hold it. This isn't so bad. Stop freaking out. This will be just fine. C'mon Larry, you've been to the US, you came back, and you've had so many crazy experiences at work already. Compared to that, this will be easy. Get a hold of yourself."

I took a swig of vodka from the minibar and made my way to the exhibition centre where I met up with our engineering team. They were putting our booth together, and it looked great. Then my interpreter arrived, and she would assist me in all my conversations throughout the day. Potential customers from the State buying agency began pouring in. We worked all day and, to my great relief, it went well. One of the most influential buyers from the buying agency spent half an hour at our booth. He had the power to buy.

When I got back to my room, there was another message waiting for me. Paul Brooke reminded me that I would have to attend a party that evening on my manager's behalf at the British Embassy. There would be invited guests from the State buying agency, and my job was to schmooze them and get a commitment for a meeting with them to discuss our products. One week ago, my job had entailed rushing all over the South of England on crowded buses and trains (and occasionally in the Hillman), and now my new job responsibility was to attend cocktails and dinner at the British Embassy. I pinched myself. Could this really be true?

In the cab on the way to the embassy, looking smart if I do say so myself, I remembered Bucharest was known as *"Le Petit Paris."* I recalled how the second most common language spoken in Romania was French. God, I wish I had paid more attention in my French classes when I was in school. The architecture of the buildings was marvellous. Neglected, yet still marvellous.

At the British embassy, I was greeted by the commercial attaché. They did an amazing job connecting potential customers to companies like the one I was working for, AMF. He guided me through the magnificent building to the reception room, made all the right introductions, and never left my orbit the entire evening. The guests from the buying agency who I had met at the exhibition showed increased enthusiasm for our products, and in turn my confidence increased, but it may have had something to do with the vodka shots I was consuming. The head buyer, to my amazement, gave me his card and said he would be in touch to discuss our equipment. Hopefully he meant the auto-jig and not my bottom that he had squeezed as he left.

That night, I slept like a baby.

1976 was the beginning of the next few years of jet-setting all over the USSR and the rest of Europe. My friends back home began teasing me that I had become a spy! While I wasn't having all the epic silver-screen exploits of Ian Fleming's fabled spy, I had my own adventures, alright.

On another sales tour of the Soviet Union, I remember flying to Vienna to meet my French engineer, Jacques, who had driven from Paris in a van containing three of our automated textile machines to exhibit in Cluj, Romania. We would share the drive from Vienna. The following week, we would drive back to Budapest, Hungary for a symposium where I would be the keynote speaker.

As we arrived at the Hungarian border, we handed our passports to the border guards, but they wouldn't let us cross. Instead, we found ourselves huddled by the side of the van as they began searching it from head to toe. They barked at us, glared at us, and even tried taking apart our textile machines. After three hours, I was flabbergasted. "What on earth are they looking for," I kept muttering. I approached a German guy who was also waiting at the border and when I asked him if this was normal, he told me,

"Do you have any cigarettes?"

"Yes, I do."

"OK, to cross this border quickly, put some money in the cigarette pack, and offer the border guard a cigarette. Then you'll see yourselves out of here in no time."

As I rolled up the notes and put the cash in the cigarette packet, I had a vision of a long prison sentence spent in a Soviet jail and all that it might involve. I had never bribed someone before so it took me a while before I mustered up the courage. However, after another 90 minutes stood in the cold, I gave in and offered the cigarette pack to the guard supervising the inspection of our van. Seconds later, we were merrily driving down the road inside Hungary.

Hours later we crossed another border into Romania (this time without delay), and we entered into another world. Gone was any vestige of modernity, and our van bumped along decrepit roads, swerving to avoid potholes, people and cattle.

Watching the people as we drove slowly past, the men wore faded overalls, and each one chewed on something - tobacco, a cigarette, a blade of grass, and the women wore coloured handkerchiefs tied around their hair as they stared back at me. It seemed like I was transported to the 1800s.

Jacques had been driving for many hours. It was beginning to get dark, and there were no street lights; the most we saw were oil lanterns in the window of the occasional cottage. He asked me to drive the last hour. He was very tired and didn't want us to have an accident. Driving through the suburbs of London had been a challenge for me and now I was driving with cattle crossing the road, no lights, no signs. What could go wrong? After just a few minutes of my driving, Jacques became absolutely hysterical. "Arrêtez! Arrêtez! Tout de suite! Larry, imbécile, are you trying to kill me? Maintenant, maintenant. Arrêt Larry!" I turned to see him pumping his foot into the floor, I laughed, "There is no point, there is no brake on your side." "Si vous plait, arrêtez!" He went crazy so I slammed on the brakes got out of the van and said "You bloody drive." We swapped places and we didn't speak another word. Finally, we arrived in Cluj, Transylvania.

I had never been to Transylvania before, and all night I tossed and turned, imagining Dracula crashing through my hotel window. In the morning, I rushed to the bathroom to check for fang marks! I was a twenty-five-year-old top salesman, and I still had nightmares about a fantasy creature I was pretty sure wasn't real.

After a successful exhibition we began our return journey. We arrived in Budapest, another city of beautiful architecture. Again, much of its glory had faded due to the Communist control of the country taking its toll, but it was still a marvel to see. The city has two parts: Buda and Pest, and I was staying at the Hilton Hotel, which was the most luxurious hotel I had ever stayed in, and was literally built into the rocks overlooking the River Danube. I dropped off my luggage and came back downstairs to see the city before the symposium began. After speaking with the concierge, I booked a tour guide to take me around the city, especially to see the Jewish sites.

Minutes later my tour guide arrived, and we were off. He introduced himself as Stephan and asked me what I wanted to see. I told him that I would like to learn more about the Jewish history of Budapest. My great-grandparents had fled to England from Eastern Europe, and I was intrigued to see how they might have lived. He knew exactly where to go, and we spent the next few hours criss-crossing the Jewish sites of Budapest. This would be the first of a tradition of mine to hire guides to show me the Jewish history each time I visited a new city in Europe.

Stephan showed me the Budapest Ghetto set up by the Nazi regime. He told me how, after the Holocaust, the Jewish community had begun to rebuild. I gleefully remarked how stunning the view was from our vantage point atop the river. As I turned to glance at Stephan, I noticed him trying to hide a sad look that had crossed his face.

"What's wrong, Stephan?"

"Nothing's wrong, sir."

"Stephan, it's OK. What is it?"

"Well, I don't want to spoil your day Mr. Gould, but it was from this same vantage point that the Nazis commanded their henchmen to line up the Jews by the edge of the Danube and shoot them into the river." It is estimated that up to 20,000 Jews were shot along the banks and their bodies thrown into the Danube.

For the rest of my trip, I couldn't get that out of my mind. Stephan was a Jew just like me, and he had to live and work in the shadow of one of the greatest evils of all time. He also told me that he was very careful not to tell people he was Jewish as anti-Semitism was still high in Hungary. The day spent with Stephan pushed me to decide to become an activist in helping fellow Jews in the Soviet Union.

My life now grew into a new pattern, one week in France, one week in Germany, two weeks in Spain and Italy, four days in the Netherlands, two weeks in Leeds, and so on. Altogether I was responsible for 27 countries and I visited 17 different countries during my time with AMF and now I was back for a further trip to Bucharest. It was always more nerve racking for me working in a Soviet Union country mainly due to the fact that in most countries in Western Europe, we either had an office and staff or an agent, so I was usually greeted by a member of the AMF team who lived in the locale and where they had often done much of the groundwork. My job was mostly to help close the deal and when necessary work as a liaison between the Leeds headquarters and the local office. However in the USSR, I was pretty much on my own, and the main support came from the commercial attaché at the British embassy. These guys were unsung heroes and many companies made great progress by using this fantastic service.

In 1978, Jews were still being oppressed in countries all across the Soviet Bloc, and were scared to openly practise their faith. Most Jews didn't have freedom of movement within the USSR or a legal way to leave, but nor did anyone else. However, Romania was the only Soviet country to allow Jews to emigrate, but freedom came at a price. $25,000 to be exact. This money was to pay back the Romanian government for the public education the country had given its Jewish citizens. I remember from my various trips to Romania that there were posters all over Bucharest for the Israeli Airline, El AL, advertising flights to Israel, but hardly anyone was buying tickets. It was impossible to get a visa, and very few could afford it.

The more I thought about the condition of the Jewish population in Romania, the more it bothered me. I had grown up thinking that I came from a poor family but, as I got to see the conditions these people lived in, I realised how much wealth we had in the West and how lucky I had been to be bought up in the UK. I met people who were my age and unlike me, they had no plumbing, no medical attention, and most importantly, no freedom.

Three weeks before I was due to leave for my Bucharest trip I was invited for dinner to my friend Sharon's parents. Her mother, Daisy, was a real character and she herself had been born in Bucharest and had managed to leave as a teenager and get to the then Palestine before the Nazis arrived. Daisy knew I was going back to Bucharest and asked me if I had time, she would really appreciate it if I could meet her cousin's son, Alex, who was my age. She had never been back since before the war and wanted me to find out how her family were doing. She had received some letters from her cousin but was sure that he would not dare be critical about the regime in his correspondence for fear of reprisals. I gave her the details of the Hotel I was staying to send to her cousin and suggested that Alex should leave a message for me when I arrived.

The day before I was leaving, Daisy called me with her cousin's telephone number so that I too could contact him. As I was to have a free weekend I made contact with Alex soon after my arrival and invited him to my Hotel. He seemed very nervous when we met. He had hinted to me on the phone that meeting a foreigner in a tourist Hotel could lead to an arrest. I had heard this before and also that many of the Hotel staff would inform the secret police if they were suspicious. Three days later I was in his apartment and met his father.

When we arrived to their apartment, I noticed that a *mezuzah* was affixed to the inside of their doorframe. A *mezuzah* is a parchment on which is written a passage from the Torah placed in a case and hung on the doorpost. It is supposed to be affixed to the frame of the door of the home, and when I inquired why their *mezuzah* was affixed to the inside, the father replied that he didn't want to draw attention to the fact they were Jews.

On my first night back in Leeds, as usual, I arranged to meet all my friend at the Pub, the Chained Bull. I couldn't wait to meet them and share my adventure and especially my encounter with Alex and how we had to be careful, and how afraid he was to be in a Hotel with a foreigner. I told them about the *mezuzah* and what a struggle life was for him and his father. Sadly they just weren't bothered and couldn't really see how it affected them. That old feeling came back about being an outsider and their reaction made me feel distant. I was surprised how uninterested they were in the suffering of people living under Communist control.

When I spoke to my Mother she said I need to be more tolerant as I had been lucky enough to see for myself and feel what it was like and they had not. I was quite shocked at her unusual lack of sympathy for my point of view.

The next day I had arranged to go to the Walden's apartment for dinner and debrief. Unlike the night before this audience eagerly awaited my news on the family. Daisy was very quiet as I spoke and I know that it must have been hard for her to be reminded of how they were suffering and how many of her other family members had not even survived.

I told Sharon and Daisy all about it and how I had found out that Alex's biggest dream was to emigrate to Israel. I must've become overly emotional about how unfair it was that people like Alex couldn't afford to leave the country. About three months later, I was delighted to hear from Alex that the money had been found by the family and he hoped he would be able to leave Romania shortly. Weeks later, I got word that he had made it to Israel but actually decided to make a visit to England to see his family and me in Leeds.

I told Sharon he could stay in my apartment while he decided what to do. He was amazed by my relatively modest apartment and this made me realise how lucky I was. He couldn't get over my multiple sets of clothing. He would take my clothes all the time, not in a dishonest way, but because he was a like a kid in a candy store. At first, I ignored all my missing trousers, shirts and cufflinks. I was happy to have helped him. Thankfully, Alex was an academic scholar, and I was grateful that he decided to return to Israel.

CHAPTER 13

Russian Spies

To my friends, I was "The Spy" and I even had to laugh at how I had gone from a shorthand secretary to an international smuggler. My company needed the services of interpreters for many of the business meetings we had with various clients. The interpreters were always attractive women. The attachés at the British embassies we visited instructed us not to put ourselves in any compromising situations with our female interpreters which could later be used as blackmail. I was single so this wasn't so much of an issue for me as it was for the married guys, but the frequency with which we kept getting warnings about these girls made the rumours that they worked for the KGB seem all the more plausible.

I travelled to meet with clients and network all over Europe, staying in 4 star hotels. One of my biggest contracts in those days was working with a Soviet buying agency to purchase auto jig machines which made small parts of Soviet army uniforms such as epaulettes and pocket flaps in a factory outside of Brno. For those trips, I was assigned Nadia who became my interpreter each time I visited Czechoslovakia. She had big, dark brown eyes, long dark hair, and was sweet and cheerful. She also had that alluring shy, yet responsive way of communicating. She wore skirts and jumpers, nothing fancy. I'll never forget her very sensible, brown lace-up shoes which seemed incongruent for someone who was so pretty. But then again, this was the Soviet Bloc and that made her even more endearing. But I always had a fear that I would be compromised, so I kept my guard up.

After a long day working at the Exhibition Hall, I took her out to dinner. When I went to pay for it, she began to cry. I asked her what was the matter, and she put her finger to her lips and said, "Let's go outside and talk," which was code for be careful what we talk about in a public place. As I helped her with her coat, and we left the restaurant, my mind was racing.

"Maybe now will be the time she finally convinces me to defect and work for the KGB".

We walked aimlessly around the city, but all she confided in me was the reason she was upset. The price of dinner was the same amount of money she earned in three months. She shared with me how poor her family was and her dreams to make her life better, despite the fact that both of her parents were doctors. As she talked about her wish for freedom, I wiped away a tear from her face, I wanted to wrap my arms around this beautiful, wounded creature and tell her it was all going to be all right. But a part of me kept telling me to be careful, "It could be a trap." But as we walked under the star-lit night, the air seemed to grow warmer around us, and we got lost in our conversation. My eyes furtively glanced at hers, our fingers brushed against each other, and I suddenly forgot how exhausted I was from the day's work. As we finally made our way back to the hotel, I walked her to her room and told her how magical the evening was. She looked up at me with her big brown eyes, and I felt my body being pulled toward her. A part of my mind screamed, "This is the compromising situation they warned you about," but she was so vulnerable, so pretty. Plus, I also had to admit there was something deliciously sexy about the chance she might actually be a spy. I gave in and that night inaugurated my relationship with the spy who loved me.

The months passed, and I regularly received letters from Nadia, but my schedule was taking me to other countries. I never did find out if she worked for the KGB or not. She wrote to me that she was applying for scholarships at colleges in England as there was an exchange programme between the UK and Czechoslovakia, but I didn't think much of it, until the day when I was in my flat in Leeds and heard a knock at the door. I opened it and was shocked to see Nadia standing in front of me with a large suitcase and even larger smile on her face. I clumsily hugged her and invited her in. She told me all about her acceptance into a university in England on a full scholarship giving her the chance to now pursue her dreams.

Looking back, I think my imagination got the better of me because I was very cold and unwelcoming to Nadia. I had let the spy jokes from my friends and the spy rumours from my colleagues create this film in my head that wouldn't let me see a more accurate and ordinary depiction of reality. I also now had a girlfriend, but I do regret being cold with her. I never saw her again. Nadia, if you're reading this, I want to apologise. You didn't deserve to be treated so badly, and I could have handled it so much better. Unless, of course, you were an actual KGB spy in which case I'll just say, "Well played!"

The Nadia episode seemed to highlight to me that my life was torn between "Larry the world traveller" and "Larry at home". Once again, I wasn't fitting in to the societal norms of my peers, and it was beginning to show. Travelling all over Europe became a doubleedged sword. I was excited by some of my adventures and wanted to share them with my friends, but I soon learnt that their lives were so removed from mine that I was in danger of becoming a show-off, so I stopped talking about my trips, and they stopped asking. Once again, I felt I no longer fitted into their social life, and they no longer fitted into mine.

One night I was back home and had gone out with my friends to a disco. One of my close friends, Richard Brown, who also was a world traveller and opened a company in New York City, leaned over and told me point blank, "Larry, you have to stop sneering at the people here and criticising them. They don't have the opportunity to do what you're doing."

It shocked me. In an instant, I realised that my adventures had made me both more worldly yet lonely and out of touch. "How do you cope living in these two different worlds?" I felt the words slip out of my mouth but I knew that, if anyone would understand, it would be him. As the music blared in the club, Richard leaned towards me and I could smell his beer breath. "When I go to New York, I feel cool. But when I come back to England, I have my friends here, and I just enjoy them for how they do things. You have to stop comparing the two. Just enjoy life!" In that moment, I felt like his "kick in the teeth" made me realise; I was lucky to be living these two lives.

I had always been a workaholic and enjoyed working like some of my friends enjoyed studying. Working was my studying and I had the capacity to do a lot of work. It may not be admirable, but it's like oxygen to me. It's something that I don't just like to do, but need to do. Even today, my life is ruled by my to-do lists and reminders. But I don't resent them or feel pressured by them. On the contrary, if my task list isn't replenished every day, I feel panicky. So I was enjoying my heavy travel and work load, but, as time passed, I started to realise more and more how my two lives just weren't matching up. I enjoyed working hard, but I wasn't having any steady relationships. As I began assessing my situation more, I realised that the harder I worked, the more successful I became. I was making more deals and more money for my company, but I still wasn't earning great money. And the worst enemy of a great life is a good life. I was comanaging two lives but neither was leading me to the great life I envisioned for myself deep down in my gut. The truth was, I wanted to be my own boss.

One night, I was at the pub with my friends, Andy and Richard. Richard said to me, "Larry you have always done so well in your jobs and have been promoted, now it is time to start your own business." I told them what I had been thinking about, but I didn't have the capital. "You tell us your idea and, if it sounds good, we'll invest so you can get started." I then spent the rest of the evening sharing my ideas.

It was 1980, and during the Thatcher period with 142 companies going bankrupt every day, but I still allowed myself to think about starting my own business. I felt a wisp of that same feeling of liberation as when I had told Uncle Cyril I was leaving America. But most of the time, I wouldn't allow myself to really think seriously about their proposal.

A secure income, prestige, and travel was something I wasn't sure I wanted to give up, but I was also overwhelmed by their generosity which they continued to offer. Months passed like this, and one night, I got another proverbial kick up the backside. I was coming home from a trip and was going to visit the girlfriend I had at the time. I wasn't so keen on her, but the relationship was convenient. I would stop at Duty Free each time I travelled to pick her up a bottle of Chanel No5. When I arrived at her place, and she saw the bag with perfume, she blurted out, "Larry, I'm drowning in all the perfume you get me. What I really want is a relationship with someone who is here all the time." I must have said something about doing better, spending more time together and being serious about commitment because she smiled from ear to ear and said "OK, let's go tell my parents". I felt like a deer in the headlights and shot out of that flat faster than you could say wedding bells. That night she called me, but I let the answering service pick it up. "You've reached the phone of Larry Gould." The next afternoon, I found a parcel in my post box with a note, the note read, "Larry, stuff you and stuff the perfume!"

As I laid awake in bed that night, I thought "Is this going to be me?" I couldn't figure out how I had allowed myself to reach a place where my love life had slipped and the word "commitment" seemed synonymous with the word "settle". "Something has got to change". The next day, I called Andy and Richard and told them to meet me. When they arrived, I was so scared that I would talk myself out of it, that I pitched them my idea without even saying hello.

"Look guys, I've been thinking about your idea of helping me start my own business."

"Yeah, and?"

"Well, I know shorthand, secretarial work, and employment agencies. Employment agencies don't have products or inventory to stock. It's a service-based business. This is something I can do and do well. My experience with AMF has taught me the importance of companies speaking to their customers in their own languages, and I'm also certain that if more companies took the trouble to communicate with potential customers in their native languages, then they would substantially increase business. I know that is true from my own experience, and I am sure there is a huge market for translations. Would you guys want in if I start my own employment agency and translation company?"

They loved the idea, but told me they needed to think about it and would get back to me. The next day, I went to see an accountant Brian Sochall who happened to be a family friend to run the idea by him and he said, "Don't have two partners". I tried to argue that I needed both of them because they were both my friends, but he interrupted me.

"Look, if you want to have a chance at succeeding here, you've got to pick one partner. And you should pick the partner who is richer and can afford to lose. It's as simple as that."

I huffed and puffed but, at the end of the day, I realised he was right. When Andy and Richard came back to me, I had to pick one of them and tell the other I wasn't choosing him because he wasn't as rich and would suffer more if, in the unlikely event, I were to fail. Although it was logical, it did affect my relationship with Andy when I picked Richard as my partner. I hadn't even started on my own, and was already ruining relationships. Being an entrepreneur is definitely not for the faint of heart.

The night before I started my business, I sat on my bed and prayed to God to help me succeed. I was totally panicked. I was leaving a glamorous job full of adventure to start my own business in a time of recession when hundreds of new businesses were filing for bankruptcy every day. If any of my old bosses had called me that night, I would have gone back to them in an instant. But the phone remained silent, and sometime during the night I finally drifted off into a restless sleep, dreaming of vampires, KGB spies, and big bags of Duty Free perfume chasing me down the streets of Budapest.

The next day, I used the £5,000 that Richard gave me to register and open Link-Up Services Ltd. It was April Fool's Day, 1980.

CHAPTER 14

Becoming an Entrepreneur

I was grappling with the seismic transition from working for a company to owning a company.

In my past jobs, though I was concerned about the success of the companies I worked for, I had no responsibility for staff or paying invoices, taxes, etc. I did my job, got my wage slip, and went home. Owning my own company made me realise that, in order for me to succeed, I had to relinquish the delicious taste of the stability of the same monthly predetermined wage slip. The hardest decision was to break free and start my own business. The fun part was registering the company, renting office space, and buying furniture, yet I worried because I was spending borrowed money. I would need to become adept at managing a variety of skills to build my business. Perhaps most importantly, I had to make the commitment to push forward, no matter the circumstances. That was my new reality.

Whilst I had emotional highs and lows and many sleepless nights, it never crossed my mind that I wouldn't succeed, maybe it was because that wasn't an option. It was scary to put my flat and my ego on the line. I constantly told myself that too much fear would paralyse me, yet a little fear would be a great motivator.

Even today, I sometimes lie awake at night and wonder what would happen if I were to lose all my wealth. I'm not brave or stupid. I make plans. I think of my options. I embrace life and consider success the ability to say in the face of failure, "How can I turn this around?" and then say, "Wow, I wonder what exciting thing I'll do next?!" My antidote to the fear is knowing that I will fail at some things and knowing that I will pick myself up and continue on.

With a few pages of paperwork, a few signatures, and registrations, I was in business. I became the CEO of "Link-Up Services" on April 1st 1980. The ongoing navigation of the ups and downs of my fledgling company would truly test my resolve.

I thought I'd been smart by making a deal with Richard where he would own 50% of Link-Up Services, but wouldn't be involved in any of the day-to-day operations. He personally guaranteed the bank for £5,000, which made him the sole person responsible for paying back the loan if the company failed. The bank agreed to match his £5,000. It didn't take me long to realise that I had made a mistake in how I set up my salary. AMF paid me £8,000 a year, plus bonuses. Richard and I agreed that I'd take £5,000 a year, which would cover all my basic needs.

In reality though, I was investing more into the company. I would be spending more time growing the company, yet we were going to split the profits 50/50. Even though he was a silent partner, splitting the profits would have been fair had I made an agreement with Richard that, as the company became profitable, my salary would increase at least to what I was earning at AMF. The frustration for me was that Richard did not agree to a salary increase agreement and, like many companies giving loans which are high risk, he was possibly right. I was left with the frustration of the situation, and what it in turn did to me was to motivate me to go it alone; and I really do think if Richard had agreed to the salary increase, the partnership would have certainly lasted much longer. In no way do I blame Richard; he kept to his agreement and indeed was very supportive.

The moral of the story: know thy worth. I should have been more forceful and negotiated an agreement so that when the business became profitable my salary would increase. I have always kept this in mind when negotiating deals with some of my executive staff. If the company is doing better, they will be rewarded with bonuses, or commission.

My flat was on the edge of a beautiful park and the night before the business was to open, I sat on a park bench. As a cigarette dangled from my mouth, my mind whirled with all the unglamorous aspects of running my new small business. Gone were the days where I would be able to fly off to foreign countries, attend business meetings, visit a range of factories, exhibitions, and embassies. Now I had to buy desks, stationery, and everything else a fledgling recruitment business needed. I also needed to buy a car for the business so I got a seven-year-old mustard-coloured Vauxhall Viva that had definitely seen better days. It was the only car I didn't crash.

As I took a drag on the cigarette, I looked up at the sky in frustration. I realised there were so many aspects of the business to keep track of. I also realised that I hadn't put together a detailed budget. I suppose having access to £10,000 made me feel comfortable. I added up in my head what we had already spent and took into consideration the salary I was taking out each month and employment costs. During the monthly meetings at AMF, we only had to show our expenses and projected sales. I was overwhelmed, lonely and scared.

So I sat up straight, took a deep breath, and screwed up my eyes really, really tight. I said to myself, "When I open my eyes, I will see something that will show me it was just a dream and tomorrow, I'll be back at my job at AMF getting ready for my next exhibition in Italy."

As I opened my eyes I saw a plane flying overhead, another reminder that I wasn't on it and wasn't going to Italy.

My sister, Dianne, never made a fuss over me and, all through my childhood, she seemed irritated by my plans and ideas. Yet, Dianne always helped me and protected me where she could. The next day, I appointed my sister Dianne as Office Manager. Dianne and I created a budget. It would be one to three worry-filled months before we would earn anything, and during this period we would be incurring costs. I insisted that Dianne take a wage when we had some income. It would be a grand total of £10 per week.

To make the business appear established to candidates and clients, I rented expensive office space in the centre of Leeds. We spent more than I would have liked, but it was important that it be easily accessible. I filled the office with six new desks and chairs, as we had planned to hire more people. We had telephones, a telex machine, and two second-hand typewriters. British Telecom hadn't connected the phones so, for the first two days, we had to use the public phone box around the corner to make all our calls. Dianne and I would fill our pockets with 10-pence pieces and remember to top up before the pips.

Two weeks later, I hired Tina Blackburn, who was a bit younger than me, and had great sales experience, and joined us at a salary of £65 per week. I'll never forget seeing her struggling out of the office in her first week juggling a mountain of leaflets to deliver to every potential client in the city.

For those first few months, I supplemented my income by reaching my "Access" credit card limit, advertised as "my flexible friend". I began visiting my parents for free meals multiple times a week and developed a passion for whole wheat toast and marmalade. After four months, I realised that I needed more money, so I rented out the spare room in my flat to Harry Lew, an Australian eye surgeon. I hated losing the freedom of living alone; but his rent almost covered my entire mortgage, and the financial relief was a great help. In times of stress, I can be quite a hypochondriac, and I also benefited from his free medical advice. We're still in touch.

In order to grow the business, I had to obtain job vacancies from the companies that I was calling daily and, alongside that effort, I had to find the right candidates to fill the jobs. This was something I had a lot of experience in when I worked in London. For the first time though, I had no jobs or candidates, and the only contacts I had in Leeds were friends and family. Not enough to build an empire.

Our office was on the eighth floor of a smart corporate building, so we couldn't just hang a sign in our window to advertise our services and jobs. I was standing at the window worrying that we had no business, and Tina exclaimed, "Look at all the pigeons, maybe we can get them jobs." Tina hung flyers up all over town, and I kept calling my friends and family. For a break, we would swap jobs. The first jobs we received were two long-term temporary positions from my friend Sandra who worked in Human Resources at the Yorkshire Post. The first post was for a secretary for the business editor, and the second was for a legal secretary for their in-house lawyer. I had two weeks to fill the vacancies.

The Yorkshire Post was the best place to advertise jobs, but adverts were very expensive. We had no choice and placed the adverts, getting a great response. Two of the applicants were suitable, and we were able to place them. Even though we had spent a great deal of money on the adverts, we now had 20 candidates for other jobs. This gave us a fantastic start, as part of the job of a recruiter is to speculatively sell applicants to prospective clients who hadn't yet given us the vacancy. I can't recall anything about the legal secretary, but the secretary for the business editor was a young woman called Michele Clarke. She had just completed a qualification in bilingual secretarial studies. I had a feeling she would work out at the largest provincial newspaper in the UK.

Even though there was a recession, the fees that most recruitment agencies were charging at the time were between 12 to 18% of the annual salary for permanent jobs. I slashed my fees by 40%. Additionally, I slashed my rates for temp jobs by 20%. Due to the relatively high unemployment rates, it was easy to find available temps. A part of me worried that people would be wary of such low prices. I told myself, "Once you get started, word will spread and people will trust your service." Without knowing it, this was my first attempt to be irresistible, and it worked.

The news from the TV and papers spouted foreboding tales of increasing unemployment rates and a doomed economy, not the sort of news I needed. I had put everything I owned on the line for the company. So I got rid of my TV and scratched the letters SNIOP into my desk, "Susceptible to Negative Influences of Other People." I wanted to treasure that feeling of absolute joy I got when I placed a candidate in a job, and they turned up for work and did well. I stopped reading the daily newspapers (except for the job vacancies section), stopped listening to the radio, and refused to hang out with people who would moan and complain. My mental energy had to be positive and focused on growing the business. Some people told me I was burying my head in the sand. I told them that without the media blowing sand into my face, I had my eyes wide open to opportunity and success.

"I have everything I need", I told them. "Marmalade and toast each morning." Hunger is also a great motivator.

CHAPTER 15

The Chaining Technique

I t was 1980, and I was 28 years old. At that time, the majority of my friends were married or getting married, and many of them had children. I was behind the curve, but Link-Up Services was my wife, my child, my pride and joy. I never considered it "my business" but "the business". Even when I started to make a profit, I never felt entitled to spend it (thanks, Mum). I always put the business needs first. Believing you are entitled is a very dangerous way of thinking because it can come at the cost of the business. To this day, I consider myself an employee of "the business" and, as the major shareholder, I always make sure that my needs don't come before the business' cash flow.

Every day I prayed, "God, please help me realise that my decision to give up my well-paying job, to borrow money, to put my flat up as collateral, and to sacrifice travel opportunities is worth it."

The flyers Tina had been posting helped keep a steady trickle of potential candidates coming through our doors, but we had to continue advertising in the Yorkshire Post if we wanted to really grow. I was pleased to see they were getting us results. In business for three months, our future was looking encouraging.

Then the Yorkshire Post went on strike, the first strike in their

100-year history. Hair pulling ensued. I told Richard and Tina that I predicted the strike would only go on for a couple of days.

By the second week of the strike, it was a living nightmare. We were getting jobs, but had no way of getting more candidates. At the same time, because companies couldn't advertise their jobs, new vacancies were coming in thick and fast. I went back to the park, sat on my favourite bench, screwed up my eyes and prayed, "God, get me out of this, let me go back to AMF, send me back to Russia."

Panic put my brain into overdrive. The next morning, I remembered that when I was living in London, there was Miss London, a magazine that people would hand out at the entrances to tube stations. It mainly contained job vacancies and was free. The magazine survived purely on its advertising revenue. "Hold on a second," I said to myself, sipping tea at my desk. "If I can't advertise, that means no one else can either. I'll start my own magazine and solve everyone's problems." I suppose this was my second irresistible innovation.

I immediately told Tina I was leaving the office (she was working on her own idea of hanging up posters on lampposts all over town) and went to my printer, Malcolm. I pitched the idea that we would start a magazine together which would be handed out at the train and bus station. He would do the printing, and Link-Up Services would sell the space and deal with administration and finance.

"Look, I'll hire four temporary telesales people immediately, and you will print 10,000 copies which we will hand out on Mondays, Wednesdays, and Thursdays. We'll split the costs and profits of the whole operation, and it will be like picking apples off low-hanging branches". I told him to think about all the businesses in Leeds that were desperate to get their sales messages out to the public. "Debenhams and all the other stores will be desperate to advertise with us!" Who knew I'd be back at Debenhams again?!

We shook hands on it, and "Extra Plus" was born. My prediction was right; everyone wanted to advertise with us. I had to hire temps for my own office as we were now transformed into an advertising agency. Our small office became a circus with people running all over the place, on the phones collecting adverts, and rushing back and forth from Malcolm's print shop. Most of our revenue was coming straight from the advertisements. By the third week, we had over 30 pages of adverts. "Maybe I should stop Link-Up Services and just focus on being an advertising agency?" I wondered.

A month after our first issue came out, a deal was agreed to between the unions and the newspaper. A settlement had been reached, and the Yorkshire Post was back in print. Of course we knew the strike would end, but we hoped that our magazine would continue as there was little competition in Leeds. The Yorkshire Post is still one of the largest papers in the UK and, in one day, we lost 80% of our revenue as Extra Plus became Extra Minus. It was time to get back to the way things used to be. Although it hurt, we laid off all the staff working on Extra Plus and I sent in my adverts as usual to the Post. I received a call the next day, "Unfortunately, we are unable to accept your adverts."

I was told, "You're a strike breaker, and you created competition for us." I couldn't believe it and tried to explain that I had only created Extra Plus because I had no other choice. We would have gone bankrupt. They hung up on me. Tina thought it was crazy, my family thought it was evil, and my friends told me they'd support me in my fight against the "capitalist Goliaths." I gave myself a night to blow off some steam, and the next day rung up the local television station, Yorkshire Television. I told them what happened and asked if they would run a story about me on how I was planning on suing the Yorkshire Post for trying to squash the little guys. They liked the idea, and I knew why.

Yorkshire Television was a competitor of the Yorkshire Post. "We'll send a guy to interview you tomorrow morning."

That night, I told my friend Ben what I was doing. He was in public relations, and I thought he'd be impressed with my strategy. He heard me out, and his bushy eyebrows knitted together, and his blue eyes flashed.

"Larry, you're making a big mistake."

"What are you talking about?"

"As much as you don't want to hear this, the Yorkshire Post is a big fish, and you're not even a small fish. You're not even a tadpole. You're a little gnat. Have you thought this all the way through? You will have your two minutes of fame on Yorkshire Television, then you'll never be allowed to advertise in The Yorkshire Post again. That spells certain doom for your business."

"But, but, but, they're a bunch of bastards! They deserve to get what's coming to them."

"Larry, it's not about who deserves what. It's about how you can get ahead of this."

"Well, if I'm going to fail, I may as well go out with a big bang."

"But you don't have to. You can win this thing."

"How?"

"Try this, call up the Yorkshire Post directly and tell them that you've been contacted by Yorkshire Television as they want to do a programme about the Post ruining local small businesses. Tell them you bought a chain and a lock from the hardware store and that you will chain yourself to the front doors of The Yorkshire Post until they give you the right to advertise again." I was beginning to feel like the Suffragettes who chained themselves to Buckingham Palace in 1914.

"That's it?"

"No, this part is critical. Tell them that you want to be their friend and, if they let you advertise again, this will all go away."

I swallowed my pride and followed Ben's advice. The next week, I was not only advertising in the Yorkshire Post for Link-Up Services, but was again supplying them with their secretarial and staff needs. His advice changed my life, and I have never forgotten the lesson of "The Chaining Technique". Sometimes all it takes is to threaten to make noise and that can bring the bully to the negotiating table. I've used this irresistible technique many times against bullies, big and small. In 40 years of business, I have never needed to sue anyone.

Due to work pressures, my social life was taking a back seat. I still managed to meet up with my friends most Saturdays, but it was no great sacrifice for me to be at work. I also made time to volunteer for the Samaritans, a helpline for those feeling desperate and/or suicidal. I found the intensity of some of those calls very challenging, yet often I walked home from a harrowing conversation feeling not depressed, rather grateful for what I had in my life. I think I was attracted to the Samaritans because my Nana Cross committed suicide when I was 19. It had a great effect on my life, and I wanted a greater understanding of why someone would do this.

At Link-Up, we began to place more and more people in both temporary and permanent jobs. Whilst it's not always clever to sell at a low price my plan was to reduce the profit margin and make it more affordable for the clients to use Link-Up. The disruptive plan was that the turnover would dramatically increase and compensate for the lower profit margins. It did. My competitors were highly critical to clients about my low fees. Many thought it was not a sustainable business model, especially those I put out of business. I threw myself into the arena of not only providing a less expensive service, but a better service.

If I didn't offer quality, cheap prices would not be sustainable in the long run.

With Tina pounding the pavement and constantly calling for more business, I was spending time with potential job candidates, for permanent jobs, preparing them for interviews, coaching them in the best ways to present themselves. I also provided them with some techniques, such as preparing a list of questions to ask the interviewer at the end of the interview and also would stress that they must tell the interviewer that they really wanted the job. One of my best suggestions was that each applicant should ask the interviewer if he or she had any concerns about their suitability for the job. After asking about any concerns, I told them to use the "silence technique". It often forced the interviewer to answer that question, which in turn gave the applicant an opportunity to think about and improve their response.

On the temporary recruitment side, Tina suggested we send someone from our office every Friday with cupcakes to the offices where our staff were working. The temporary staff provided by other agencies would often then register with us because we cared enough to deliver a weekly treat.

I also created welcome packs for our clients to give to temporary staff. Normally when a permanent employee joins a company, they go through an induction programme; however, a temp is expected to immediately take on the role that they are covering for. We created booklets with information about the company and the job and even taped a 10 pence piece inside of the booklet which enabled them to use the public telephone should they need to call us (no mobiles in 1980). These became irresistible reasons for people to work with us. Because I had been a temp and suffered from not having inductions, I understood the temps' needs better than most, Link-Up Services had an advantage.

Link-Up Services was now four months old, and our business was steadily growing. We had the contract with The Yorkshire Post, and Yorkshire Television started giving us vacancies, too. I hired two new employees to do telesales and recruitment. Now I wanted to expand our in-house secretarial services and language services. I was always paranoid and because of this, did not want to rely on only offering one service, temporary and permanent placements.

I had learnt the importance of speaking the customer's language back at AMF. When I was promoted to Export Sales manager, I was sent to work in the company's Bordeaux office. Tutors in Leeds helped me to improve my French skills. Now that I had started my own company, I thought to myself, "Why don't we offer a translation service using teachers from Leeds Trinity University." Francine, who was my French tutor, started to work for us part time, managing the translation work. But then she left. I was still emotionally exhausted from the "Yorkshire Post Episode" and without Francine, I was spending all my time on the phone trying to sell our translation services. I knew it was time to employ a full-time secretary with language skills.

Tina had placed Michele Clarke as a temp at the Yorkshire Post, and she received a rave review for her secretarial work. "Not only is her work exceptional, but she's willing to accept the low hourly rates we are paying for this role." I told Tina to bring her in for an interview as I knew she could speak English, French, and Hebrew. The next day I met Michele. She was 19 years old and very shy. I offered her the job on the spot, and I could've sworn her eyes brimmed with tears.

A new opportunity arose due to the fact that British Telecom (BT) had increased the cost of renting a Telex machine by more than 100 percent. Many users cancelled their Telex service with BT. The Telex service was a forerunner to the fax and computer; it was basically typewriters communicating with each other in real time. The cost of sending a message was cheap, immediate, and international, and this service was quite profitable. Link-Up Services had to have a Telex so we then used this opportunity to offer a Telex service to other businesses. We looked through the Telex directory and contacted all the people in the Yorkshire region who had had a Telex and offered them our Telex service with an annual subscription which was the equivalent to 15 percent of BT's fee. Within weeks we were adding new subscribers daily. Subscribers would telephone in and dictate their Telex messages which we would send on their behalf. We now had Link-Up Recruitment, Link-Up Languages and now Link-Up Business Services.

There were times when we couldn't provide a temporary secretary so we offered an in-house secretarial service: Michele. Michele would transcribe letters from an audio tape. Before sending out the letters, she showed them to me for proofreading. As I checked for spelling or grammatical errors, I realised her skills were better than mine.

Each day, I was calling potential clients.

"Hello, I'm Larry Gould from Link-Up Services. I'm calling to find out what your staffing situation is, as we provide both temporary and permanent staff. What vacancies do you have?"

"None."

"We also translate and interpret into and from the major European languages. What languages do you use in your business?"

"Never mind bloody foreign languages. We speak bloody Yorkshire!"

"OK. Well we also provide Telex transmission services, copy typing, audio typing, photocopying, and a mailbox service."

"Do you also sell sandwiches," he asked?

"No," I replied.

"Well, that's probably because you're a very busy lad."

After that conversation, I created divisions under Link-Up Services: Link-Up Recruitment, and Link-Up Languages. I took great care to only sell one part of the business at a time and to ask far more questions than I did in that dreadful attempt at sales.

About three months later, I was checking over an audio tape Michele had transcribed for a new client, Michael Rivlin. He had an amazing idea to create rental offices and offer short-term agreements, rather than a lease.

I thought about how to expand on his idea and called him. He told me that he'd returned from the US where he'd seen a new business. They rented office space, monthly lets, and even rented desks. Before signing the contract to offer our business services in their buildings, Michael and his partner Roland Stross wanted to meet the person who would be managing these services. Michele went from being a temp to my secretary to the new manager of Link-Up Business Services, all in a six-week period. Michael and Roland were very excited and asked us to move into their building for three years, rent free. This was a massive benefit for us as we were about to sign our lease for a second year, and additionally we would have built-in clients in the new serviced office accommodation.

In 1981, Work Space opened. Michael and Roland provided the rental space and desks. Renters would have access to all our business services. It was a great partnership. Little did I know that over the next few months, Michele would make Link-Up Business Services 45% of our annual revenue as I would make the same deal with five other work spaces.

After three years, we made the decision that the return on investment was not worth it. Whilst this division was profitable, it took up a lot of manpower and resources.

One of the hardest things in business is to give up something that is working well, to sacrifice it in the hope that the transfer of assets and time to another part of the business will create better returns. I decided to focus on recruitment and language services.

CHAPTER 16

Love Is In the Air

Some people think that when it comes to the dating game, you're either a James Bond natural or a guy who sits on the side lines waiting for Cupid's arrow to strike. But the truth is that we all have our good days and bad days. Some of us are better looking, funnier, more sensitive, more athletic, and the list goes on. As much as I'd like to forget the awkward moments of my own dating game and pretend I was 007, that's not the truth when I think about my dating and relationship resume.

In the late 1970's Turkey was in turmoil, and I was sent to Istanbul by AMF. Bombs were going off regularly, yet my company was going to supply equipment to a factory, and it would be quite a substantial sale. They sent me to meet a senior representative from the World Bank who was co-financing the deal.

Istanbul is the only city in the world that straddles two continents, and during the meeting he invited me to dinner that evening at a posh restaurant overlooking the geographical spot where Europe and Asia meet at the Bosporus Strait.

I was nervous as it would be the first time I would be meeting a banker in a social setting. Very few guests were there due to the civil unrest in the city. Seated next to him was a stunningly attractive woman. She looked like a combination of Sophia Loren and Elizabeth Taylor. I couldn't take my eyes off her. Turns out I didn't have to as she was his interpreter for the evening. Veronica. Even her name was beautiful.

I ordered onion soup and, as I sipped my soup, my eyes flitted back and forth from this boring bank guy droning on and on about God knows what to this woman sitting just inches away from me. I was trying so hard to be James Bond. As I was about to take another spoonful, I had a massive sneezing fit.

I sneezed the soup all over her cleavage. Here I was, 27 years old, as red as a tomato, trying to wipe soup and snot off her perfectly tanned cleavage with my napkin whilst stammering an apology. She was incredibly gracious and told me not to worry. I was praying for the ground to swallow me up. The banker arched an eyebrow at me.

I managed to regain my composure. "God, just get me through this dinner as fast as possible." The main course came and went without any problems. For dessert, they served traditional baklava. As I was finishing the last few bites, a black cat jumped up on my lap. I screamed and knocked over all the glasses on the table. "God, just kill me now." This was too much for the beautiful interpreter, and she began laughing hysterically.

The banker shook his head at me in horror. Her laughter filled the restaurant and slightly eased my bruised ego. I was so nervous I even laughed a little, then excused myself saying I had to prepare a report. I escaped to my hotel room, punched the wall, and paced up and down. I was embarrassed and humiliated. After ten minutes of berating myself, I was convinced that if the story got back to my boss that I would be fired.

There was a knock at the door. I opened it and, to my shock, there she was. Veronica laughed and placed her hands on her hips. Words came out of her mouth, something about wanting to make sure I was OK. I think I managed to mumble that I was fine. "Wait, hold on, she wants to come in. Yeah, sure. Come on in. What for? Oh, she just wants to make sure I'm OK. Didn't you say that already? Oh, her hand is grabbing mine. Oh. Is this really happening? Oh, my God, she's locking the door."

The truth is that the dating game generally wasn't much fun for me. Sandy, my American girlfriend had dumped me. Suzanne my Australian girlfriend, slept with some guy the night before we were due to return to Leeds.

Prince Charles and Diana were getting married, and the entire country was celebrating. I invited all my friends over to my flat to celebrate. I told Michele she should come. I wasn't sure she would but a few hours later she appeared at my door. I had never seen her in jeans before. My friends had been drinking and were making all the requisite jokes about good-looking secretaries. I tried to shut them up before she got within hearing range. The next day at work, I found myself finding excuses to call her into my office.

Even though Michele and I spent every day together at work, I was completely blind, as usual. She was extremely hard working and a major contributor to the business, yet I'd tease her daily about her personal quirks. She was adorably clumsy and had a habit of dropping things all over the place. She was quieter than the girls I had known in the past, but she definitely wasn't quiet when it came to work. She'd correct me all the time when necessary in her gentle way.

On Fridays, Michele's father would come to collect her from our office. I guessed he was only about ten years older than me. He would ask how she was doing, much like a parent would ask a teacher.

I didn't realise how attracted to her I was becoming. The actor Darnell Lamont Walker once said, "Sometimes our walls exist just to

Larry J Gould

see who has the strength to knock them down." I didn't let myself see that the great walls of Jericho around my heart were tumbling down due to the grace and kindness of this sweet young woman.

An entire year passed, and I still hadn't made a move. Michele had told me that her parents had a home in Israel and one day came into my office and told me a group of her friends who were in medical school were going there on holiday. She wanted to join them and asked for permission to take an extended holiday. "Of course," I told her.

Michael Rivlin, one of the owners of the office building walked in to my office for a meeting. "What's new?"

"Oh, nothing much. Michele is excited because she's taking a three-week holiday in Israel."

"Aha, I bet she's going to go to interviews whilst she's there."

"Pardon, what do you mean?!"

"I know her parents, and they told me she is planning to emigrate to Israel!'

I was shocked. I had never felt anything like this before, not since Miss Silver had got engaged to the Chief Rabbi of Belgium. It was the most miserable three weeks without her. The entire time I kept replaying memories I had of her: the time she first came in and dazzled me with her sparkling green eyes; the time she showed up at my party for the royal wedding; the time we went to pick out uniforms for our office reception staff, and I accidentally caught a glimpse of her incredible figure in the changing room.

When she returned, she looked even more adorable. The Middle Eastern sun had coaxed out all the freckles over her fair skin, and I couldn't take my eyes off her. I had no idea how to handle this situation. But, thankfully, someone died. Sadly, someone passed away in the Jewish community whom we both knew. I heard they were observing the traditional *shiva* mourning period and asked if she was going that evening. She was. Before God could resurrect the dead, I quickly blurted out, "Would you like to come with me?" Our first date was comforting the mourners.

I picked her up in my Vauxhall Viva. The driver's seat kept falling back, but we made it to the *shiva* house. Afterwards, I asked her if she wanted to grab a pizza. She said "OK!" She couldn't finish her pizza and politely asked, "Do you mind if I don't eat the whole thing?" I couldn't figure out why little things like that made me smile so much when I was with her. All week long, I couldn't stop thinking about her. She was my employee, and she was ten years younger, only 19. I didn't know what to do.

I called her into my office. "I'm invited to a dinner party this weekend, and I have no one else to take. Would you like to come?" James Bond would have cringed. Michele shocked me with her response, "As all my friends are on holiday, I may as well come with you. I have nothing better to do!" Not a very gracious offer and not a very gracious acceptance, but I felt a wave of sheer excitement.

That Saturday evening, we were invited for 8.00pm but I had to pick her up for the dinner party at 6.00pm as my friend lived 3.5 miles away, and I expected it could take two hours to get there. On the Sabbath, observant Jews don't use a car until after sunset, so I left my car on the next street to Michele's home. It had been years since I had dated a girl who lived at home. It was embarrassing for both her parents and me. We all just stood there while we waited for her to come down from her room.

We walked to the dinner party, and the entire way I couldn't work out if I should hold her hand, put her arm through my own, or wrap my arm around her shoulder. I hadn't thought about things like that since I was 14 years old.

Michele held her own gracefully throughout, although it was a strain for her as many of my friends were at least ten years older and talking about babies, curtains, and carpets. I was certain after this evening it would be the end of our budding relationship! After dinner, one of my friends drove us back to my car and, as I had had more than usual to drink, I asked Michele if she would drive me home and bring the car back the next day.

True to her word, she returned my car. It had been snowing all morning, and I was so excited to see her at my door. We spent the next few hours just talking and talking. Before we knew it, there was a blizzard blowing outside. "Wow," I said, insisting it was going to be too dangerous for me to drive her home. She rang her father to tell him she didn't think she'd be able to make it home. That's not exactly the thing any protective father wants to hear, his daughter stuck at her boss's home. He told her emphatically, "Michele. I'm coming to get you. Go wait outside by the park gate."

As we waited outside, the snow danced all around us. I think I was joking around too much because I slipped and fell. Just like a Hollywood romantic comedy, she bent down to help me up, slipped, and fell down next to me. We were giggling and laughing. I looked over at her lovely face and knew in that moment that, no matter what happened, I was going to marry her. Continuing the movie, two strobes of light shone down upon us as her father pulled up in his car.

A few days later, I took her out for dinner in Harrogate, not for pizza but a real dinner. Afterwards, we were walking back to the car, and I kept trying to build up the courage to kiss her, another thing I hadn't worried about in a long time. Finally, I leaned forward, bent her head back into the crook of my arm, and kissed her. I had never felt anything as thrilling and wonderful as when she kissed me back.

Six weeks later, I asked her to marry me.

The First Ethiopian Bar / Bat
Mitzvah, 1997, Jerusalem, Israel

Larry and Michele with Prime Minister
Ehud Barak, 2000, Manchester, England

Larry with Ethiopian Bar Mitzvah boys, 1997,
Great Synagogue, Jerusalem, Israel

The reunion with Uncle Cyril,
2000, Dix Hills, New York

Joshua's Bar Mitzvah, 1997,
Harrogate, England

Ilan's Wedding, Hilton Hotel, Tel Aviv, Israel

Julian and Joyce Gould's
Wedding, 1948, Chapeltown
Road, New Synagogue,
Leeds, England

The end of a beautiful evening, Ilan's
Bar Mitzvah, 2002, Hale, England

Larry at Fir Tree School, aged
10, 1962, Leeds, England

Larry's Family Bar Mitzvah
Photo, 1965, Queens Hill
Avenue, Leeds, England

Larry aged 7 with sister Dianne,
1959, Leeds, England

President Larry Gould, B'nai B'rith
age 15, 1967, Leeds, England

Dr Larry Gould, Leeds Metropolitan
University, 2011, Leeds, England

Larry and Michele's Wedding,
1982, Leeds, England

Larry's Bar Mitzvah, The Great
Synagogue, Belgrave Street,
1965, Leeds, England

Larry's 66th Birthday, 2018, New York City

Larry's Mum, Joyce aged
17, 1944, Leeds, England

A slimmed down Mr Irresistible,
2019, Leeds, England

Larry, Michele and all the children, Dalya and
Adam's Wedding, 2012, Hale, England

CHAPTER 17

The Proposal

On the Monday after our first date comforting mourners, I have to admit, it felt a little awkward in the office. I received a call from the owners of the building, Michael and Roland, who invited Michele and me to their office for a meeting. Their office was on the top floor, and we were on the ground floor. The lift in our building was old fashioned. I had to pull a lever and, sometimes if somebody touched the lift gates, it would stop between floors. I still maintain that I did it by accident, but when the lift stopped, she looked quite startled. I found the opportunity too irresistible. Almost in slow motion, I took her in my arms, looked in her sparkling green eyes, and kissed her. Over the next few weeks, we went on all sorts of dates to amusement parks, a pool resort, and dozens of dinner dates.

These days, everyone makes a big deal about the proposal but that's not how things were done back in 1982. I didn't want to propose over dinner at a restaurant. "What if she says no? Then it'd just be awkward." I'd already been dumped at a restaurant in New York and sneezed soup all over an interpreter. After dinner, in what was becoming our favourite restaurant, The Flying Pizza, we came back to my flat. I was very nervous. She asked me what was wrong. I couldn't get the words out of my mouth, "I'm just stressed about work but let's not talk about that, let's just sit down and relax." I put on one of my favourite albums, Carole King's Tapestry. As the song Will You Still Love Me Tomorrow played, I got on one knee, and I told her that I would love her always. "Michele, in the short time since we've gone out, I've loved you more than anyone else. Will you marry me?"

It was a good thing we weren't in the restaurant because she smiled coyly and said, "I need to think about it." After letting me suffer in silence for five entire minutes, she answered, "OK, then, yes!"

We sat there and talked about how we would share the news with her parents. She was nervous about what they would think. She asked me to let her get used to it before saying anything to her parents. We agreed that the following Sabbath, she would walk to the synagogue with her father and tell him that I had something important to talk to him about and would visit on Sunday. She told me she was surprised when her dad didn't probe any further. I kept thinking that her mother and father were only 12 and 15 years older.

On Sunday morning, I took Michele's sister Louise for driving lessons in her mother's fairly new Honda. I don't know if it was my poor teaching or her bad driving, but she crashed the car. An hour later, I asked Michele's parents for their daughter's hand in matrimony.

I was 29 years old, had my own business, my own flat, and had even managed to maintain a good reputation, notwithstanding all my travels and exploits. I was considered a good catch, but the first words to come out of their mouths were not congratulations or fantastic rather, "Who have you told?" I was taken aback. "Um, well, I've told my parents." Her mother looked at me and tugged on her dress. "First of all, Michele is only 19. We think she should wait. She's just too young." I leaned back in my chair. I had been hoping they would bring out the celebratory bottle of champagne. I tried to keep my cool and asked, "OK, for how long must we wait?" Her father replied, "At least until she's 21 years old."

"21? 21 years old? I'll be 31 then. We know each other really well now. We love each other." Her mother calmly and kindly replied, "Give it time Larry."

"Time for what? To get my pension?" I replied. Needless to say, that didn't go down well.

Back at home, my parents actually did have champagne out. They had fallen in love with Michele, my mother especially. She wasn't so keen that Michele's family were religious. They were devastated when I returned home alone and told them, "You can't tell anyone." I particularly didn't want to tell my grandparents the bad news, but I had to as I didn't want them to tell anyone in the community. Nana Gould never got over this rejection of her grandson and never forgave them.

The next few weeks were difficult. I told Michele, "I can't come to your parents' home anymore. It's just too insulting." Michele was really strong and six weeks later, she confronted her parents. "I really love him. I really do. And we want to get married soon." Her parents relented. Our parents met each other, and it was cordial. We planned a big wedding and invited all our friends (unlike my Bar Mitzvah). Of course, it had to be a very religious wedding and was officiated by Rabbi Angyalfi, a scholar from the Chabad.

Now that Michele and I were married, I was over the moon with joy. Of course, I would have to adapt quickly to the fact that my new bride was both very observant and very spiritual.

We wanted to be able to invite Michele's parents to come to my flat, and it was necessary that our kitchen be kosher. To do this, we employed the help of the rabbi's wife, Rebbetzin Shoshanah Angyalfi. The following week, the rebbetzin, and Michele's mother came to help make my kitchen kosher. My mother had never kept kosher and even though I had studied all about it at Hebrew school, I quickly realised I needed an extensive refresher course.

The rabbi's wife went through my entire kitchen asking questions about the history of every pot, pan, and piece of silverware. So much of the crockery and china that family and friends had given me as house warming presents were quickly piling up on the counter tops to be given away. It could not be made kosher. I watched as the rebbetzin pulled out a box and began throwing items that could be "koshered" in the *mikvah* (ritual bath), and I was about to say something. But I looked at Michele's happy face and bit my tongue. An hour later, the rabbi showed up with a blowtorch, a bloody blowtorch, and koshered my oven. To say I was traumatised is an understatement.

A big challenge for me was that Michele couldn't travel on the Sabbath. She never asked me to do anything, and I never asked her to break any rules. She'd attend services in the synagogue each Shabbat but never once asked me to come with her. If I didn't join her, she wouldn't say a word. But when I did join her, she was so pleased. She made becoming a more observant Jew into something pleasurable rather than a punishment, but it certainly took a while.

We began celebrating all the Jewish holidays. At first it was difficult to observe the rules, but Michele had a way of making the holidays so much fun that I'd look forward to celebrating. She'd invite over dozens of friends and family and cook up a storm. On Hanukah, she printed out song sheets that had both the Hebrew and phonetic English. Our home became a place of joy, light, and happiness. I couldn't believe it when I found myself humming the Shabbat and holiday songs under my breath. Pretty soon, I was coming up with my own ideas to make the holidays even more irresistible. When Michele heard me saying I was looking forward to the next Shabbat or holiday, she smiled and kissed me.

After getting married, the social dynamics with my father were slightly better. Now that I had my own place and my own business, it was hard for him to find something to nitpick with me. When I started my business, he was still working, but 18 months later he retired. His factory was bought out, and he was 61 years old at the time. Because of my mother's illness, he had been very careful about retaining insurance coverage and also had a nice pension waiting for him. But retirement bored him. Whenever I'd come around to visit, he'd ask a bunch of questions about the business, and it almost always led to an argument. He'd slam the door on me as he walked out of the room, and I'd turn to Mum who would just shake her head sadly.

However, my sister and I knew he was bored and Dianne suggested we recruit him to work a few hours a week. I reluctantly agreed. My recruitment business was growing, and we now had 80 temp staff working in 27 different companies all over Leeds as clerks, secretaries, drivers, etc. We weren't sending out pay cheques because some of the temp staff didn't have bank accounts. We needed someone to go to the bank, put cash into pay packets and deliver them to the appropriate businesses. I offered the job to my dad. He loved it (although he made sure to negotiate harshly on the pay, which he didn't even need).

Not long after he started, I realised it wasn't going to last. He'd go every Friday to drop off the money, and then he'd return to the office and just hang around watching people work. I'd ask him, "Hey Dad, can I get you anything?", and he'd smile smugly, "No, I'm just watching. Just watching." I tried to tell him that it made my employees uncomfortable but he'd just walk off grumbling. My Mum scolded me, "You're really hurtful to Dad!" I was flabbergasted. "Me? Me hurtful? Mum, he's just sitting there watching my employees work. It's awful!" I was a grown man, irritated that she made me feel ashamed. I hadn't been scolded like this since she caught me taking sixpence from her purse for ice cream. A few days after that conversation, my Dad quit. It took some time for my Mum to forgive me.

CHAPTER 18

Many, Many Changes

A ten-year age gap forced us to talk about it at the beginning of our marriage.

"Michele, in just five years, I'll be thirty-five."

"Larry, don't worry. We have so many years ahead of us."

"I know. I'm talking about wanting to have children with you. I know we both want it, but thirty-five is the cut-off age for adopting children here in the UK. Once I hit thirty-five, we won't legally be allowed to adopt."

"Adopt? Why are we talking about adoption?"

"What if we wait to try to have children and then find out we can't? These years will go by fast and, if we wait, it might be too late for us to adopt."

Whenever we'd visit my friends, Michele was thrust into nappies, bedtimes, and baby talk, something Michele did not enjoy. Her social circle were still travelling around the world without a care. I was cognisant of my age and beginning to worry.

I convinced Michele to stop taking birth control pills and told her it would still probably take us months, if not years to conceive. Three weeks later, at just 20 years old, she was pregnant. I was thrilled and relieved. Michele was in shock.

I had a great relationship with my sister's children James and Hannah and couldn't wait to be a dad. Although we were still paying off the cost of the honeymoon and the recent move from my flat to our new home, we were on the fast-track to the next level of married life. Michele was sick all the time, and adding to the misery was a terrible spell of hay fever. She tried to be positive, while coping with changes to her body which she hadn't expected would happen so soon.

My stress levels further increased as I began considering the financial implications of having a child. I had barely broken even after two years in business. With Michele pregnant and throwing up all around the office and on the way to and from the office, I would often have to stop the car and hold back her hair whilst she was sick. I knew she would soon have to slow down and not work as much, but she never did and worked up to the week before giving birth.

Luckily, at the same time, there were developments at the business. I had begun placing more and more temporary staff at the head office of the discount store, Poundstretcher. The directors planned to take on their main competitors, Littlewoods and Woolworths, by acquiring 120 stores which were previously DIY shops and converting them into Poundstretcher stores. As the stores were country-wide, they realised that their biggest challenge was finding managers to run them.

At this point we had over 60 temporary staff working in their warehouse and offices. As the directors got to know me, they became aware of my retail experience. They asked me to attend an urgent meeting and shared with me that they had now acquired the 120 stores and over the next few months would complete a refurbishment programme. They realised that the managers of the DIY stores were not the right calibre to manage Poundstretcher stores, and they asked if I could handle the recruitment. I told them that there were two ways I would do it. The traditional way would be to advertise, but my recommendation was that I would obtain the salary levels for Woolworths' and Littlewoods' store managers and poach them. I stressed it would only work if they were willing to pay a higher salary. At first they weren't sure about it, and I asked them, "What other reason would make these managers leave a huge, successful company like Woolworths?" After a week of negotiations, they gave me the contract.

My charges were substantially higher than my normal fee as I would need to travel the length and breadth of the United Kingdom while continuing to run my business. I adopted a number of creative approaches to gain access to the managers. The best approach I found was to go into a store and ask to speak to the manager about an important, private and confidential matter. This worked in many cases, though one manager thought I was a private detective as he had been having an affair and was relieved when I wanted to speak to him about a new job. I told each manager that my client knew that they had an excellent reputation and would like to offer them a position.

I often stayed in some very deprived towns, suffering from the effects of 1980s deindustrialisation where the stores were expected to be most successful. I was away from home, staying in fairly grotty B&B's, feeling sorry for myself, while Michele was at home throwing up and dealing with pregnancy alone.

I now had to drive thousands more miles, not something I relished with my rubbish driving, navigational expertise, and knack for crashing cars. At least I had traded in my orange monstrosity for a new car. However, the pleasure of the new car had been somewhat spoilt when Richard said, "Just remember that 50% of your car belongs to me!" As if I wasn't nervous enough about driving.

It was the straw that broke the camel's back. During a trip to

Scotland, I kept replaying what he said over and over. "Here I am, slaving away to build this business into new markets and doing *all* the work while Richard is just sitting back on his laurels reaping the rewards, even though that was our agreement. Is this how it's going to be for the rest of my career?" If I had been single, I think I would have just accepted it and gone with it but I was now a husband and soon to be a father. The need to be a provider crystallised my need to chart my own destiny.

I would never have had success without Richard. He believed in me and encouraged me to fly on my own, and I'll never forget that. Yet sometimes a partner is for life and sometimes not. There's no strict rule about business partnerships but if there was one, it would be to regularly evaluate whether your partner is adding value or not. No matter how you feel about them, the ability to control your own destiny may exact a price. If I had stayed with Uncle Cyril, I would have had electric curtains and all the status it represented, but without the freedom and independence I really craved.

Around Christmas time when I was wrapping Christmas gifts for our clients, including bottles of whiskey, wine, and boxes of chocolates, Richard casually asked me, "Do you have any bottles left over for yourself?" I replied, "Yes I think I have ordered four more bottles than I need." "Great, I'll take two, and you keep two." "Thank you," I said, but he must have missed the irony in my voice. Our relationship had started off with him being an investor, a giver, but that dynamic had now changed to where he was now just a taker. Yes, he was entitled to be a taker; he had invested a lot of money and had been very supportive in the first couple of years which I had greatly benefited from and appreciated.

As much as I didn't want to make our friendship awkward, he could no longer be my business partner. I had to break up with him. It was a simple calculation: I needed to be in control of my own life and destiny. The only partner I wanted and needed was Michele.

I took Richard out for a drink and praised him profusely for being a wonderful partner and wonderful friend, which was genuine on my part. I laid it all out on the table and told him how I needed to come into my own. To my surprise, he smiled. "I knew this day would come." I breathed a sigh of relief, thinking it may not end as badly as I thought. He then drained his glass of whiskey, paused, and told me, "The only thing is, I don't think you can afford to buy me out." If he hadn't been my best friend, I would have stopped at this point and waited until I had taken legal advice on my position. But he was my best friend, and I heard him out. He wanted £45,000. I had no idea if this was fair or not. I told him that I would speak to my bank and get back to him. That night I couldn't sleep, racked with guilt. Without him, I wouldn't have a business. Now he owned me. Did I deserve to be owned? No I deserved to be my own boss. The next day, during lunch, I went to the bank for what I thought would be a simple stop on my road to independence.

My bank manager at Barclays, Mr. Fewster, had been incredibly supportive, and I think he was both amused and pleased how I called him every time I had got a new client.

"Look, Larry, I admire you, but you're barely making any profit, and I wouldn't consider lending you this amount of money in a million years to buy out his shares. Look at it this way, I've never met Richard, but the value of your business is nowhere near a justifiable £45,000 buyout."

I was disheartened, and he must have seen that. He leaned forward and said, "Right now, you're overtrading and probably need a larger overdraft from the bank. You're only a couple of years into your business and have trouble with your cash flow. But I believe in your business, and I believe in you. I think you have done a tremendous job. We would consider lending you money for the buyout if the amount was right.

And by right, I mean much, much less. I think you need to talk to your accountant and get advice."

Two days later, sitting in Brian Sochall's office, I still thought that if Richard had asked for £45,000 that is probably what I would have to pay. When Brian repeated the same words as Mr. Fewster, I asked "Well, how much do you think I should pay?" Brian pushed the copy of my accounts aside, looked me straight in the eyes, and said very slowly, "Larry, are you mad? Are you even listening? Your business is not worth it." I tried to push back but he cut me off. "Larry, *you* are the business. It's worth nothing without you. For him to demand that amount is preposterous. He's overvaluing the business." Once again, life was teaching me the hard way how important it is to "know thy own worth." Sometimes it can be advantageous to understand it is less than you thought. I asked Brian what amount would be fair to give to Richard. "So low that I don't think you should tell him unless you have a lawyer and myself present." I felt like I was preparing for a divorce.

A few days later, Richard and I were seated in a conference room flanked by our accountants and lawyers. I started the conversation by saying, "My bank manager won't support any loan to buy you out and neither will my accountant." Richard was expressionless, which made me even more uncomfortable. He was my best friend. I finally managed to spit out my offer. "I'd like to offer you £5,000 payable over the next three years." Richard shook his head, "That is ridiculous." But my accountant had prepped me, and I said, "Just know that I have set up a new company. I will leave the current company, and you will be responsible for all the debts. All the staff will come with me to my new business because they don't know you. So I suggest you leave the room and speak to your advisers before you reject my offer." I could only be this strong because I kept thinking about my pregnant wife and the staff who depended on me. It was the most uncomfortable conversation in my entire business career.

We took a break, and I was visibly shaking. I vented to Brian, "This is the most terrible, repulsive thing to do to a best friend." He grabbed my arm. "He has his £5,000 back in bonuses, and now he is getting another £5,000 which is not a bad deal in just over two years. Larry, get over it, and grow up."

When we reconvened in the conference room, Richard's response was quick. "I agree to your offer, but I want 2% over the base." I had no idea what that meant and my accountant interjected, "Yes, we'll accept that." Minutes later, I was walking out of the conference room with my company and my independence, but without my best friend.

When the news broke regarding our deal and split, to my surprise, our crowd of friends took sides. The gossip was less than complimentary to me, and I was socially demonised. Friends told me that I was disgusting. "How could you do such a thing? Where is your gratitude for what he's done for you? We think you are getting above yourself."

I had gone above my station. Even today, 40 years later, at events in Leeds, some of Richard's friends still will not speak to me. I dealt with it by throwing myself more into my work and, thank goodness, there were some positive moments to distract me. Poundstretcher had been absolutely delighted with the work that I had done and during a meeting with the directors, I mentioned that I had worked on a project with Asda some years ago – the Race to 100%. It was a training plan that covered all aspects of a retail manager's job, and I suggested to them that this programme could be adapted for Poundstretcher. I was not pitching the idea for me to deliver, but merely raised it as an issue for them to think about. The directors were very excited and asked me if I could come back and make a presentation to them and if I would be able to deliver the programme. Luckily I had saved all of the documents relating to the programme.

They booked me for 60 days of training over the next six months. Whilst I was flattered, I was very concerned as 60 days away from the business would be a minimum of 120 days as once again this meant traveling all around the UK. So rather than saying no, I decided to outprice myself. In 1982, I charged them £650 per day, plus expenses. Of course, they balked at the price, but I explained to them my concerns for my business. To my utter shock, joy, and disappointment they accepted the proposal. It was fantastic money, and the reaction I was getting was tremendous. This model proved so successful that I have used if for many other companies; and in 1991, I received the highest award from Prince Charles at the National Training Awards. I have the photo to prove it.

I was literally working day and night with huge amounts of travel to boot. Add to that, the stress from the break-up with Richard had really affected me, and I was not in a good place. Instead of my usual positive self, I started to complain about everything. One day, Michele turned to me and said, "You must regret marrying me, Larry." I was shocked, "Oh my God. How could you say that, I absolutely adore you." A tear slid down her cheek as she said, "Before we got married, you were very positive and excited but in the past few months, you're always moaning and complaining all the time. I must be doing something wrong …" I cried out, "No, no, it's just about work. It's not about you at all." She looked down at her hands. "Still, I wonder if you're happy being married to me and having a baby." She broke my heart when she said that. But she also broke the spell.

I remember breaking down, crying, and saying, "I'm just scared. All the nasty feelings about the break-up with Richard have been eating away at me. I'm just so worried about making the right moves for you, me, and the baby." From that moment on, I have credited my successes to her because she never tolerated me being down or unduly depressed and, at the same time, she has always been there to simply listen and support me.

Three months after the deal with Richard, we were blessed with the birth of a boy, Joshua. The birth was quite normal and uneventful, except for the nurse catching me taking a hit of the high-dose of gas and air to make sure it was working. As Michele and I looked down at our son's big, wide blue eyes, we were ecstatic. Two years later, our daughter Dalya came along and then, soon after that, our youngest son, Ilan. I was 37 years old and a dad of three.

CHAPTER 19

The Birth of Irresistibility

I had spent so much time with accountants and lawyers, consumed with trying to buy Richard out and getting the bank to lend me money against my house, that I was fearful I was neglecting my business. The minute the meeting was over with Richard, my sense of purpose changed. Now it was time to put the focus back on the business.

As a child, my biggest dream had been to have enough money to buy a sixpence ice cream cone. Even though I was still worried, I had my own company, my own family, my own house, and my own huge mortgage. I felt like I had it all. I smiled at that little boy standing at the ice cream van.

The first thing I did after the meeting with Richard was go straight to the newsagents and buy everyone at the office a Cornetto ice cream (large). Walking into the office with a box of ice cream cones, I called my team of eight to a meeting. "Right folks, I've now bought Richard out. We are now in control of our future, so let's get down to it."

"What are we going to do differently?" I asked the staff to give me a word that would be applicable to all our stakeholders. "Fantastic," "professional", "amazing", "extraordinary", maybe we were getting somewhere with extraordinary. Then suddenly our newest member of staff, Sheila, shouted out, "irresistible."

I stood up and wrote IRRESISTIBLE in capital letters on a flipchart. I asked Shelia to look it up in the dictionary. "Too tempting and too attractive to resist."

"Tell me what's irresistible about the services we provide?" I was met with blank stares and continued, "Look, no matter whether we're talking about customers, suppliers, or even our own staff, we need to go above and beyond. What we're trying to identify is why Link-Up is irresistible. Our job is to find out the irresistible reasons why someone would want to work with us, why someone would want to be a customer, to be an employee, or contract worker and even a supplier to the business. Why is the future with Link-Up irresistible? For example, I want to ask suppliers, contract workers, customers and most importantly, you, what is irresistible about Link-Up?"

The team loved it and, not only did it guide our creative juices in the right direction, but just using that word made us believe we really could be irresistible. On that same day, my team came up with some ingenious ideas that we implemented straight away, and a number of those ideas have sustained us over the last 40 years.

This was followed up by another irresistible solution. In addition to office workers, we also supplied temporary factory workers. Many were workers from countries such as India and Pakistan with limited English language skills. Whilst the Yorkshire Box Company in Bradford would accept limited English speakers for repetitive work, such as assembly line and packing, often workers didn't understand key information about the company, and its rules and regulations. So we created welcome packs and translated them into the appropriate languages.

My sister Dianne came up with the next irresistible solution and asked why our recruitment consultants were not speaking to HR departments in other companies. I implemented this, and our recruitment team had great success by explaining the difference between Link-Up and our competitors which was that we either translated their staff handbook or created one for them and translated it into the appropriate languages. One of our first customers was British Steel; we created a handbook and translated it into Bengali, Gujarati, and Urdu.

In 1983, we began coming up with more and more irresistible services for Link-Up, and things began to take off. But inspiration is only the seed of any successful idea. It takes perspiration to bring it to fruition, and my motto was and still is, "the harder you work, the luckier you get". I began working every hour possible to put this motto into action and, I have to admit, I also demanded a great deal from my staff. At the same time, my friends were taking their business profits and going on holidays and buying bigger homes, whilst I kept reinvesting all my profits back into the business. Instead of causing me to burn out, hard work energised me. I made more sales calls, read more, and pushed more to become even luckier.

With the "Irresistible Model" as our vision, the "Hard Work Ethic" as our engine, and "Irresistible Customer Service" as our fuel, Link-Up had the perfect trifecta that propelled the business forward. I kept seeking ways to make products and services that were better than anything else offered on the market. Michele was spending more and more time back in the office, which I was very happy about. Even with the massive mortgage weighing down on me, it was a really happy time. We also moved to Sandmoor Lane which was one of the poshest streets in Alwoodley. The first time I walked into our new house, I was overwhelmed. It was another sixpence ice cream moment. I had arrived and it was delicious.

On a bright winter's afternoon, I received an urgent call from Michele's father. He wouldn't tell me what was wrong, but I could hear the grave worry in his voice. I dashed over to his house and, with his face as grey as ash, he told me Michele's mother had just been diagnosed with terminal cancer. He cried and asked me if I would be the one to tell Michele.

I drove home in silence and slipped into bed next to her. She smiled at me and said, "Dalya has finally gone to sleep. She has been really great today." Seeing the smile on her face, I couldn't bring myself to tell her. "It can wait until morning. Let her have one more night of peaceful sleep." But I couldn't fall asleep. She always knew when something was eating away at me and would make me tell her. In that moment, Michele's life was turned upside down. She was the eldest of the three siblings and the only married child, so the brunt of the responsibility fell on her. For the dark months ahead, she was constantly by her mother's side, praying for her and taking care of her. Not until three weeks before her mother passed away did her sisters know the severity of the situation.

I knew that my role was to be strong for Michele and the rest of her family. Outwardly I was, but my bouts of anxiety returned and transformed into panic attacks. My doctor wanted to give me drugs, and I told him I didn't want to put that stuff in my body. He recommended self-hypnosis but referred me to his colleague, Dr. Padwell. He trained me in the art of self-hypnosis. It was very hard at first, and with perseverance on both sides, he gave me the tools I needed to calm myself down when I was overwhelmed. On the day of her funeral, I promised myself I would use those calming techniques to be a better husband, father, and employer.

At the same time, I was in the process of purchasing a new head office in Leeds for our expanding company. Belmont Park was our home for twenty years. We were also opening more branches across the United Kingdom. In addition to my huge mortgage, I also negotiated a substantial loan to fund the expansion. By the time we had completed the purchase of Belmont Park and had opened three new branches, we were hit with the financial crisis of 1989. Again, when I had taken a leap forward, the economy was failing and interest rates were skyrocketing across all sectors. The mortgage on my house doubled per month, and interest rates on our bank loan increased from 7% to 12%.

I hadn't been this scared since I had left AMF and started Link-Up in 1980. Once again I stopped reading newspapers and brought back the SNIOP sign (Susceptible to the Negative Influences of Other People). Over the next five years, I managed to navigate Link-Up through the potholes and roadblocks of the financial crisis. I had started with only two clients in 1980, and now in 1994 had an annual turnover of $30,000,000. Life was good. I even began allowing myself to say the occasional, "Thank God."

CHAPTER 20

The Deal?

"Hello, Larry Gould speaking."

"Hi Larry, I'm Roy Smith, and I represent a US investment company backed by Michael Milken who is looking to invest in the employment industry. Is now a good time to talk?"

"Yes."

"We have been following your progress and have been stunned by how well you have done in growing your company. My investors are looking for a cornerstone company such as yours where we can grow it to be one of the UK's largest recruitment businesses. I am going to be in Leeds and would like a couple of hours of your time." I tentatively agreed to meet with him the following week. After I got off the phone call, I researched Milken and discovered he was a billionaire investor from America.

A week later, Roy arrived at my office, my whole head was filled with contradictory emotions, absolute excitement, fear of such a big change, and anxiety about what life could be like afterwards. "Calm down, this is not going to happen", I said to myself.

Roy explained that "After a lot of research we believe that the recruitment market was about to rocket and it is our plan to enter the recruitment market, and we think your business would be an excellent cornerstone."

"What does a cornerstone mean?"

"When you are entering a new market, you are more likely to succeed when building a new business that the cornerstone needs to have strong leadership and management and a profitable turnover, which we believe Link-Up has. We have a substantial war chest of $170 million and we are planning on adding a number of other recruitment companies around the UK."

He told me that they had done a substantial amount of research on me and my company and that he very much admired the way I had grown Link-Up and the great reputation it had. Without anything further he said the following magical words, "We want to offer to buy you out for $9,500,000." He also said it would be great if I could be part of this new exciting company. He went on to explain that they were negotiating with three other companies, all smaller than mine, and he felt I would be really important in integrating them into the new company.

"Pardon? Did I hear you correctly?" I managed to politely finish the conversation and told him I needed to see the offer in writing, and he asked me to give him a week. I didn't sleep at all. After three days, I received a non-binding offer.

I spent time talking with Michele and my sister. I contacted my close friend and lawyer, Michael Davidson, and asked his advice. His response, "Fucking sell it!"

The next eleven months of negotiations and meetings dragged on with emotional highs and lows, whilst I was still running the business with my sister. Having no experience selling a business and dealing with an investment fund, I surrounded myself with experts who helped me navigate through the process.

The buyers required financial information and data which created an enormous amount of pressure, completely diverting me from running the business. There were always delays which they said were due to being in the middle of other deals, buying other employment businesses. During this period, my mood was dependent on when I had heard from Roy or not, when we spoke I would be high, but after six weeks of silence I was low and depressed. Though they gave assurances and apologies, I was beginning to wonder and my senior management team was feeling insecure as well. It was my job to keep everybody calm.

Once they began the due diligence process, which was expensive and time consuming for them, we knew that the deal was going to happen. Due diligence lasted six weeks, and finally on 12th November 1996, Michele, my sister, and our Financial Director, Alistair Nichol, accompanied me to our closing meeting at the offices of the investment fund's accountants PriceWaterhouseCoopers in Manchester. On the way to Manchester, I said to Michele, "I can't believe it, our lives are going to change; we are going to be financially secure, and I'm going to have an exciting career." Michele said, "I hope we are going to go on some summer holidays!"

With a small army of accountants and lawyers, the final meeting went on for 19 hours. We were assigned a room in which to wait. Their lawyers and accountants brought in mountains of paperwork; my team of lawyers and accountants went to and from the deal room with questions and relatively small changes to the contracts.

At one point, Michele and I escaped to take a lunch break and grab some pizza. As we sat in a booth across from each other, munching on our slices, I couldn't help but think back to our first date. Michele seemed to read my mind and smiled. "Do you mind if I don't eat the whole thing?" We both laughed.

"Michele, tomorrow we're going to be millionaires. What would you like to buy with our money?"

Silent for a moment, she then smiled, "I want all my amalgam teeth fillings changed to white fillings." It had been more than a decade since we met, we had three children, and little things like that still made me fall in love with her all over again. We returned to the marathon of signing papers which continued well into the night. My corporate finance advisor, Hugo Haddon-Grant, had held my hand throughout this process, becoming more of a therapist than an adviser. At the beginning of the process he told me to make it very clear that I wanted to stay with the business after it had been sold, demonstrating that I believed in the business. At only 44 years old, it was important to show that I was enthusiastic to stay. I agreed with him, but in truth, I was desperate to stay, after all Roy told me that I would be instrumental in the future of the new business. I wondered what my new role would look like.

Even though it was exciting, I was about to fall asleep when Hugo came into our room. "Larry, we are onto the final document, which is your contract with them."

I sat up to listen, and my heart was beating fast. This was it. I looked at the contract and said to Hugo that there was a lot of changes to the contract, he seemed embarrassed and uncomfortable.

"From what I gather Larry, they only require your services on a hourly and daily basis which will give you a lot of free time, and you are not tied to them which is great!"

"Oh, oh, is that good?" I said in shock.

"Yes of course it is, you only have to work when you want."

"So I don't have an actual role."

"No. Isn't that exciting?"

"Yes, I suppose," I lied.

An hour later, I was fast asleep on the sofa in reception. "Psssst. Mr. Gould?" I looked up through bleary eyes. A PWC rep informed me, "The bank is about to confirm the transfer of the purchase price into your account. For some people, this may be an anti-climax." I grinned, "If some people think getting millions is anticlimactic, they don't know where to shop."

Moments later, a trolley with champagne and crystal glasses was wheeled into the room. At that moment I decided that if I didn't have a role in that business, I didn't need to lose any more sleep so we began the drive back to Leeds, Michele was driving of course. It was 4 o'clock in the morning and the snow was beginning to fall. I called my mother from the car.

"Larry, it's 4 o'clock in the morning. Is everything alright?"

"Mum! Mum!" I burst into tears, and told her, "I just became a millionaire!" There was silence, and I held my breath. "Larry, that's wonderful!" I could hear my mother's pride and happiness. Then my father came on the phone, "Lepke, I am so proud. I always knew you could do it." Whilst I was pleased he was happy for me, at this moment my mother's pride meant much more.

I had finally done the deal. I had gone from Larry the School Drop-Out to Larry the Multi-Millionaire.

The next morning began like all other mornings. The same sun rose in the east and shone into our bedroom. The same alarm clock began chirping at 7:00am. The same thoughts flooded my mind as I opened my eyes. "Get up. Shrug off that tired feeling. You've got to get to work." I stopped when I realised I didn't have to get anywhere.

My body was habitually used to getting up and stressing about our mortgage, the business, winning and losing clients, and covering the bills. But on this morning, I had a fortune in the bank. I could finally allow myself at the age of 44 to relax. In just one day, I had gone from all stress to no stress. I sunk back into my pillow and closed my eyes to savour the delicious feeling of freedom! I managed to shrug off my disappointment that I wouldn't be involved in the new company.

I had caught the dream I had been chasing ever since I was that little boy from Seacroft. My friends had degrees from Oxford or Cambridge and had become professors or barristers. Yet I was the one who had finally broken free of the rat race of life and had accomplished what millions of people sought every day: the power to do anything I wanted.

I didn't need to go to work today. I didn't need to stay in Leeds today. I could go anywhere I wanted, and do anything I wanted! It was overwhelmingly fabulous! I let the feeling wash down from my forehead to my wiggling toes.

As I lay there in bed, hands behind my head on the pillow, with the warmth of pure contentment, I began to realise it wasn't just about the money. It was more than that. It was also the recognition. Not just from my family, friends, and society, but recognition from myself. I had finally affirmed it to myself. It was not the constructs of life that defined me; it was who I believed I could become.

Just before the deal was done, the buyers asked if they could have a photograph with me. I was feeling exuberant and obliged with a big smile and thumbs up. I never imagined that the next day, the Daily Mail newspaper would be churning out thousands of copies, breaking the news of my success. The business page ran the title "GOULD SELLS OUT FOR £6 MILLION" with that photo. I knew Michele was going to be horrified about publicising how much money we were now worth. But between you and me, I was bloody delighted.

I looked over at Michele, and she was still sleeping peacefully. I wanted to kiss her but she looked so content and so delicate. For the next hour, I just lay next to her and kept wanting to pinch myself, "Is this real?" Finally, she woke up, and the first thing she did was smile and kiss me. "Larry, we need to explain this to the children. You're going to be home far more often and because of the awful photo you let them take, it could be in the paper, so you need to tell them before they find out from their friends at school."

As usual, she was right. Josh was only six weeks away from his 13th birthday, Dalya was ten, and Ilan was already seven. After they got ready for school, I gathered them all at the breakfast table and said, "Mum and I have something to tell you. We've sold our business." It sounded weird, even to me, so I quickly piled on, "But we kept the small language company." Michele and I held each other's hands, interested to see how the kids would react.

Dalya was the first to respond. "Daddy, are you happy about it?"

"Yes, Dalya. Very happy. Because now I can spend more time with you!"

She cocked her pigtails to the side and smiled, "Well, then I'm very happy about it as well."

Sliding off the chair, she came around, and gave me a big hug. I squeezed her back, and she asked, "Now, can I have some porridge please?"

Ilan got right down to the nuts and bolts. Between mouthfuls of porridge, he shouted, "Dad, how much money did you get?" I said, "Oh, we got quite enough." He munched for half a second before looking at me with a grin, "Can I have a computer, Dad?" I said "No, because I'm not working anymore and the money has to last." Of course, that was a ridiculous thing to say on my part but I felt I had to say something.

"Oh, you're so mean, Dad!"

Josh was old enough to have come around the office a lot and had the most understanding of what was going on at the business and what the sale meant. He burst out crying, "But what's going to happen to all the people, Dad?" I chuckled and calmed him down. "Don't worry. They're not being sacked. They're going to stay and work for the new owners of the business." He immediately felt better. "Oh, that's good, Dad."

For the first time in years, I was able to stay and see my kids off to school. I kissed them on the head as they left, smiled, and wondered, "What do I do next?"

The newspaper was posted through the letterbox. Michele was horrified about the photograph as I predicted. The first call was from the bank manager at our bank, Barclays, who congratulated us on our good fortune. He wanted to send over a wealth management expert who would advise us on how to "cope with the new situation." Something about what he said irked me and, as I hung up the phone, I realised what it was. This was the same exact expression one might hear in England if a doctor informed you that you had a serious illness. Coping with my new situation was definitely not the language I would have used. I laughed, "I've only been a multi-millionaire for a few hours, and they're already treating me like there's something wrong with me."

Three hours later, a smartly dressed banker arrived at our doorstep. "First of all, I'd like to congratulate you. Whilst what happened to you and your family is exciting, it can be very challenging. Mr. Gould, the most important part of my job is to advise you in how to invest your wealth. But I do much more than just that."

"Oh, really?"

"Yes, our bank has advised a number of lottery winners and people who have suddenly come into a windfall of cash similar to yours. It's integral to my position to share with you some of the common issues they face. Consider that now you have the freedom to do things which your friends and family can't even dream of."

He paused for dramatic effect. "So, in my professional opinion, I'd advise you to consider giving your close family some of your money in order to soften the blow on them." This seemed ridiculous and patronising. "I've worked 26 years to get here. If people find it hard to cope with me, that will be their problem, not mine. It's all very new. Thank you very much for your advice. I'll be in touch." The first person to reach out to congratulate us after Barclays was no one.

After breakfast, I decided to go to my office as there was still the language company, and I thought it was important to go and see the staff I had worked with and thank them for their contributions.

The truth is that having wealth does change you, no matter how sincere your intentions. For starters, you now have the finances to do things that others can't, like buying a big house with cash, putting in a swimming pool, travelling anywhere you want or even something as simple as not having a schedule that locks you down. You're never ready for the intimidation your newfound wealth will have on your friends.

I had to learn the hard way. I remember talking to one of our close friends and feeling happy to share that we booked our first family getaway in years.

"Where to?"

"Taking the kids to Thailand."

My friend scoffed, "We can't even afford to go to the seaside, and you can go to Thailand."

I was speechless. We'd been friends for years and always shared our family plans and trips with each other. I wasn't prepared for a response like that and started to see this type of resentment more and more frequently in our friendships. People would ring us up and say, "Hi Larry, we've booked a table at this new restaurant tonight. Will you both join us?" I remember saying, "Can we just go out for pizza? "We *can* afford it, you know!"

I believe there's a cultural component to all this. In America the attitude is, "If my neighbour can achieve the American dream, so can

155

I!" This attitude may not be as vibrant as it once was, yet I still see it as a shining virtue of American culture, yet in the United Kingdom, there remains the remnants of class system bias which lingers on in the cultural psyche. From the proletariat to the royal elite, there exists clear distinctions between the working class, middle class, upper middle class, upper class, and the aristocracy.

One can be barely surviving with no money but, if you come from an aristocratic bloodline, you'd sneer at someone like me. On the flip side, the working class can also be snobs. Although, one of my friends sent me a greeting card after finding out I sold the business with the words emblazoned on it, "Nouveau riche is better than no riche."

As time went on, Michele and I realised that many of our friends didn't know how to act around us. Aside for my anthropological theories, there were some people who were just bitter and resentful. We realised that if we had ever been in dire need in the past, these friends would have come rushing to our aid. They would have been fabulous to us and helped in our hour of need. But in our hour of triumph, many of our friends abandoned us. I spoke to some of them, and I was shocked at their reactions. Two close friends told me, "You fucking left school at 15, we went to university, worked bloody hard for our degrees and it pisses us off that you now have all this money."

We wanted to keep our circle of friends but their spoken and unspoken comments made us feel apart. However, we knew that if we lost all of our money, they would be there for us. We started to refer to them as our foul weather friends. It took us some time to accept this and, when we finally did, we had to let them go.

Around the same time, I was forced to deal with another disappointment. I was 44 years old, and I had loved building and working at Link-Up. Now, I had nothing to do. I had kept Link-Up Languages, but it was still only doing around $350,000 a year. My sister still managed all the day-to-day operations and didn't need any help from me in running the company.

At the signing, the investors told me that they would retain Belmont Park and the staff. Two days later I went to the office, and I received a call from the HR officers of the acquiring company. The day after the deal, they decided to close the Leeds office, and 170 people would be made redundant with immediate effect. I found out an hour before they told the staff. It was heart-breaking to see many of my staff in such a terrible state, coming to my office in tears. Many were angry, asking why they had been laid off when I had told them otherwise. Contrary to what I had told Josh, I was forced to watch as my business was being dismantled and kept hearing about business decisions which I would never have agreed to.

This was the first time since I was 15 years old that I didn't have a job and, although I couldn't yet articulate it, I was feeling a deep sense of purposelessness. A week later, I walked into the office at 7:00am with a piping hot mug of coffee. I sat down in my chair and turned on the computer. "Wait, something's not right."

It was the quiet. From my office, next to the receptionist, I used to be able to hear Susy joyfully answering 600 calls per day, "Hello, Link-Up, how may we help you?" "Oh my God, what have I given up?" I shook my head as a wave of guilt crashed over me.

"Larry, you're a horrible person. You've just become a millionaire and you're complaining? How dare you feel sorry for yourself!? You've reached the dream so many want. What has happened to you is nothing short of amazing!" But, I rebutted myself, "It's too quiet. What am I going to do with myself now?"

Then the phone rang, and I was delighted that somebody wanted to speak to me. It was Marty Davis, the managing Director of United

Jewish Israel Appeal (UJIA). He was visiting England on a fundraising trip, and I am sure he had heard about my change in circumstances.

"Larry, I'm in Leeds. Can I come and see you?"

"Oh, I don't know."

"Larry I'm only here for a few hours, and I have something really exciting to tell you."

Twenty minutes later, Marty appeared in my office, slightly out of breath. Before he even sat down, his mouth was already moving. "I have a very exciting proposition for you."

A few moments later, I was sitting up in my chair with excitement. Five minutes later, I was on the phone with Michele.

"Michele, Marty Davis from UJIA is at the office. I'd like you to come and meet him."

"Oh Larry, I've lots to do. I really don't want to come to the office. Whatever donation you want to give will be fine with me; just make sure it is focusing on a children's project."

I repeated in a more firm voice, "Michele, you need to come to the office. Now!"

"Larry, why?"

I took a deep breath and, knowing how excited she was going to be to hear it, said slowly, "Because we're moving to Israel." The phone went dead, and minutes later Michele appeared in the office. She was slightly out of breath but her eyes were sparkling.

CHAPTER 21

Turning Our World Upside Down

"I think you better sit down; I have some news to tell you, and what I am going to say will shock you." I paused and took a deep breath. Michele's demeanour changed from slight exasperation to concern.

"As you know, I was offered a job with Spring Recruitment in Los Angeles, and if you'd agreed and I left the country before April 7th, then I wouldn't have to pay any capital gains tax on the sale of the business which would save us about £1,500,000. Because you didn't want to live in America, I turned down the job. So, this is the news. Marty has offered me a job at UJIA in Tel Aviv as Director of Employment Services. I will set up eight job centres throughout Israel and focus on helping immigrants from the former Soviet Union and Ethiopia. This really appeals to me, and to be honest, so does the option of saving the capital gains tax. I know in the past you wanted to move to Israel, and I said it wouldn't be possible because my Hebrew isn't very good, but Marty has told me that in the first couple of months, I will spend most of my time brushing up on my Hebrew. So I'm willing to give it a go."

"Michele, I know this is your dream, and it wasn't mine; but sitting here in my dismantled head office, I'm left with a small language business which Dianne is running. What have we got to lose?"

"Do you really mean it?"

"Yes."

Michele was ecstatic and kept asking me if I was sure. That life-changing decision was made quickly, but one thing money had given me was choice, and if I made the wrong choice we could always come back to Leeds. I took Michele in my arms and said, "Let's do this for two years, but then I want to come back to the UK as I understand the business culture here. Whilst I am even happy to buy a home there, I must stress that we are coming back to the UK. For a moment she looked disappointed, but it was not going to stop her from enjoying the excitement as we continued to make our plans to spend time in Israel where she was happiest as a child and felt the most comfortable.

But first we had to prepare for Josh's Bar Mitzvah. I wanted to make it truly special. When we initially started preparing for his celebration, I remember going over the menu with Michele and planning a bold, extravagant reception. I wanted to splurge on my son's milestone. I wanted to make sure Josh would feel joy at his celebration.

The cost far exceeded my budget so I told the caterer we'd have the hors d'oeuvres and chicken but to cut the soup course. But that was all before I sold the company. As soon as the sale was final, my first call was to my mum, the second to Celia Clyne, the caterer. Before she even had a chance to finish saying hello, I screamed, "The chicken soup is back on!" I have never felt more triumphant ordering soup in my entire life.

We rented out the beautiful Royal Baths in Harrogate and got Josh, Dalya, and Ilan brand new clothes. We also made plans to fly to Israel the day after the party so he could have a second ceremony at the Western Wall in Jerusalem. We invited 50 of our friends and family to come with us, and we were footing the bill for all the feasts and fun trips we had organised. We were calling it Josh's Bar Mitzvah Safari!

I don't think I realised how over the top the celebration was until I received the invoice for my order of 2,000 balloons and balloon sculptures for the party in Harrogate. At first, I felt guilty and then suddenly I remembered that scared little boy looking up at his sick mum in the gallery having the most miserable Bar Mitzvah in the history of Leeds. It dawned on me how lucky I was, not only to be able to spend the money but to spread the joy. I also really love balloons.

Not wanting anyone to be distracted from Josh's big day, we didn't tell my parents about the move until a week before the Bar Mitzvah. At least, that was the excuse I kept telling myself for not sharing the news with them. The real reason was that my mother was now in her late 60s and quite frail. Whilst her multiple sclerosis had not worsened over the years, it was still debilitating. We spoke every day, and I knew that our move was going to be very hard for her.

Of course, I offered to fly my mum and dad to Israel whenever they wanted to visit, but I was concerned that my mother wouldn't feel up to making the long trip, though she did come to celebrate her 70th birthday. As I feared, when we told her the news, she cried. But, ever the lady, she kissed me on the cheeks and told me how proud she was of me. My father, in his usual sarcastic tone said, "That's nice Larry, just go and leave us now!"

Our next stop was to Michele's father. The news that I would be taking Michele to Israel was mixed. On the one hand he was sad, but on the other he was excited that we could spend holidays together as he also kept his flat in Israel. I had to repeatedly warn him not to tell my children until after the Bar Mitzvah.

At 9:00am the morning after the Bar Mitzvah party, a coach would arrive at our house where our family and friends would start our journey

161

to Israel for Joshua's Bar Mitzvah Safari. We had not yet told Michele's sisters our plan, and we didn't think it was fair to tell them in front of everyone else. So we went at 7:00am to Michele's sisters to tell them. But I never expected their reaction and still chuckle when I think about it.

"Michele, Larry. It's so early in the morning. What's going on?"

"Michele and I have something to tell you."

"Oh no! Are you two splitting up?!"

It took me a couple of minutes to stop laughing. Then Michele told them all about our plans, and they were happy for us. We rushed back to the house and woke up the children. "Hey kids, we have exciting news for you. After Josh's party in Israel, we're all going to live there!" Dalya and Ilan shrieked as if they had won the lottery. Josh calmly rolled his eyes and declared, "I know Dad. I've been reading all your faxes."

Later that day, as we sat on the plane to Tel Aviv, the kids could barely contain their excitement that they would soon be moving to Israel where they had spent many of their summer holidays. Their excitement was so infectious that we changed our plans and, on the first day on the Safari coach, I got up and announced, "At the end of this week celebrating Josh's Bar Mitzvah Safari, you'll all return home to England, but I won't. I've only bought a one-way ticket because I'll be staying here getting everything ready for Michele and the kids who will join me in five months' time. We're moving here, and I will begin working as Director of Employment Services for the UJIA." There was stunned silence, followed by applause.

Michele and I had decided that the children shouldn't make the move until they finished their school year in July. I was going to disappear from their lives so soon after only just reappearing. Suffice to say, I missed Michele and the kids terribly during the months that they stayed back home in England. But whilst the kids were finishing up their school year, I was just beginning mine.

For my first two months in Israel, UJIA had enrolled me in an ulpan, an intensive education course in Israel geared toward teaching immigrants Hebrew. Whilst my French had miraculously improved (thanks to AMF), my Hebrew was just as bad as it had been back in Hebrew school. My powers of concentration had not improved with age, and I couldn't blame migraine medication anymore. Because I got bored in the lessons, my behaviour deteriorated. I was especially badly behaved with my two new best friends, Dennis, a doctor from London who was on the run from his wife, and Jacques, a French plastic surgeon specialising in gender reassignment. Unlike Miss Silver, my teacher, Nurit, was constantly telling me to shut up and listen. I failed the first level three times over the next few months. I had just sold my business, celebrated my eldest son's Bar Mitzvah, and moved to a new country. The last thing I wanted to do was stay indoors hunched over Hebrew books.

Every morning, I'd wake up in my father-in-law's apartment in Herzliyah Pituach, a suburb of Tel Aviv, grab breakfast at the cafe down the street, and then hop into my rental car to head to school, I did miss my smart Mercedes and the chauffeur I had left back in Leeds. Israel was so intoxicatingly alive with the hustle and bustle of people and I was so excited to see everything that I honestly don't know how I made it to school. I never crashed the car. Maybe it was a miracle of the Holy Land? Once in school, Nurit tried to cajole and motivate us to pick up the language. "It's easier to learn than English!" Whilst she was undoubtedly right about that, I almost had a panic attack on the first day when she concluded the lesson by giving us homework! Even in secondary school, I rarely did my homework, and I wasn't going start now.

Of course, I had to do homework to pass my class. So what does a 44-year-old entrepreneur do to handle this? Why, delegate of course!

Every day, after school, I promptly went home, faxed my homework to Michele in England, and then went out on the town to have fun with my new classmates who ranged from 21 to 75 years old from France, the United States, and Russia. I'd come back home, see the faxes from Michele, and get horribly homesick seeing her handwriting.

Every four weeks, Michele would fly in with the children. Of course, the last thing on my mind was going to school. I'd take them to all the places I had seen, to the zoo, the beach, restaurants every night, and have adventures in every spare moment I had. Hence, another reason I failed my exams thrice. It was pretty disgraceful, especially considering that I was technically the CEO of a language services company.

Eventually, I realised I couldn't keep failing school as I'd soon have to focus all my time on my job at UJIA and speak Hebrew. I redoubled my efforts and finally passed. The whole school cheered for me when I got my diploma and even some of my friends from the first two classes I had failed showed up to support me.

I began to work at UJIA, and a month before Michele and the kids were scheduled to fly in for good, we found our dream house. Located in Herzliya Pituach, it was a magnificent home with a pool and miniature orange trees growing on all the balconies. When the kids saw it, they fell in love with it immediately. "Daddy, this is so cool!" The glass floor in the living room that looked down to the swimming pool was certainly cool. I didn't want them to go back to England, but I consoled myself with the knowledge that their next flight to Israel would be for good.

I had financial security and was about to enjoy free time with my three children whom I had hardly seen during their very early years. Luckily, it wasn't too late. My kids were still young, and if I had not sold the business, I know I would have regretted it.

They say that money can't buy you happiness. That is true but it can get you pretty close. The rest was up to me.

CHAPTER 22

Adventures Abroad

I woke up to air raid sirens. How could I have done this to my family? I got out of bed and paced; it would be two hours before their flight was scheduled to arrive. I was terrified. What if a missile were to hit the plane? Surely, the authorities will re-direct the plane. Had I been foolhardy and selfish? I looked at the five boxes I had just purchased. In each box was a gas mask.

In the summer of 1996, Sadaam Hussein was, again, threatening to bomb Israel with chemical missiles. The entire country was on high alert and the words "bomb shelters", "practice drills" and "chemical warfare" filled the daily lexicon. I had also invested in upgrading the bomb shelter in our new home and purchased special equipment which would remove chemicals from the air in case of an attack. I had also been advised to assume the electricity would also be knocked out during an attack and stocked our bomb shelter with toiletries, dry food, bottled water, flashlights, and a chemical toilet.

On my way to the airport, I was shaken out of my reverie, not by the sound of a missile but by a loud horn. Narrowly missing an oncoming articulated lorry, I was driving on the wrong side of the road! I finally arrived at the airport and rushed to check the board for any delay.

The flight was on time. My emotions high, I ran to the gift kiosk and purchased a dozen "I love you" balloons and three stuffed teddy bears. I nearly tripped over my homemade cardboard sign with the words "Welcome home Gould family, Daddy." I certainly attracted a lot of attention in the airport.

Finally the sliding doors opened and three kids rushed towards me with shrieks of happiness, followed by Michele pushing a trolley loaded with cases. There was no drug that could have made me feel as high as I did in that moment. As their arms wrapped around me and balloons went flying everywhere, I burst into tears.

Michele, the kids, and I drove to our brand new home. With my recent graduation from the Ulpan, Michele, a fluent Hebrew speaker, and the kids by my side our adventures in Israel could truly begin.

Michele and I enrolled the kids in the American International School for two reasons. Firstly, I didn't want them attending an Israeli school where the lessons would be in Hebrew. I also wanted to impress upon them, or at least Michele, that we were only staying in Israel for two years; and secondly, the lessons were all in English. Their transition would be easier.

There were students from over thirty different nationalities, cultures, and backgrounds, and my kids would have to make new friends. But when school started, they settled in more quickly than I had hoped. I wasn't worried that much about Dalya who was 11 years old at the time. She was the most academic and easy going of our three children and settled in right away, scoring the same top marks she had scored back in England. Ilan was eight years old and missed his friends, yet was very adaptable by nature.

It was Josh who I worried about. As a thirteen year old, I knew how important his group of friends back in the UK were to him. I worried what this new start would do to his academic and social confidence.

One day, his teacher called to tell me that a story Josh had written in literature class had received the highest grade in the class and, "We just wanted to share how well he is doing as we know you are concerned." When Josh came home from school, I heartily congratulated him. He shrugged his shoulders. "It's not a big deal, Dad. I'm the only person in the class who can speak English." But it certainly gave him more confidence, and I felt relieved that he was doing well.

Ilan gained a new independence that he had not enjoyed in Leeds. Despite all the frightening headlines about Israel in the paper, there was very little crime or violence in the streets. At eight years old, he was able to roam and explore with far more freedom than he could have imagined.

However, he, like his brother and sister were well aware that if the air raid siren sounded they had to return home immediately, I have to admit I somewhat traumatised the kids because I forced them to have a dry run. I sent them to their bedrooms and told them when they hear a whistle blow, they would have to make their way to the bomb shelter down three flights of stairs in the dark. I reminded them to bring their gas masks with them. We then gathered in the bomb shelter and locked the doors. We practised turning the wheel on the chemical extractor which we hoped would remove poisonous fumes. I then showed them how the chemical toilet worked, something that Dalya found particularly revolting. I don't know the long-term effects on our children, if any, but I do know it gave them and me a greater understanding for people who live under the threat of attack around the world.

Now that I knew the kids were doing OK, I really began to allow myself to enjoy the new life we had created. Since the day my children were born, I had been focused on the business first, and the family followed. I missed many bedtimes, suppers, school functions, and other opportunities to be with my children. Although I applied my work ethic to developing the job centres for UJIA, I did my best to ensure, when possible, to take my kids to school, to be there when they got home, and always have time for them. The weeks became a blur of delightful barbeques in our beautiful garden, swimming parties in our pool, daytrips around the country, and dinner dates with friends, many of whom I met in the Ulpan, many we met on previous trips to Israel, and our new neighbours. But there was nothing more satisfying than the chance I now had to get to know my children better.

It was easy for me to do this. I had money in the bank, a job I didn't really need to do, and lived in a gorgeous home with a pool in a stunningly beautiful and exotic country. When I became successful, some people told me, "You're so lucky!" But no one except for me knew the hard work and sacrifices that it took.

The sacrifice that had been most difficult for me to reconcile was the realisation that I had been an absent father. I managed 200 employees and 24 branches for Link-Up and worked hard to make it all happen. I convinced myself I was doing it for them, but it was mostly for me. I didn't want my kids to live in the conditions in which I grew up. I would be a failure unless I gave my children the choices my sister and I never had, no matter the cost.

The cost was that I usually only saw my children on the weekends. And even then, whilst I was reading story books to them, half my attention was on the mortgage, the problems at the office, and all the stress that came with being my own boss, not to mention falling asleep whilst reading them a bedtime story. So I made up my mind that my time in Israel would be the exact opposite. I would organise my work so I could go on trips, hang out at the house, and do whatever I needed to do to get to know my children for who they were and, of course, spend more quality time with my lovely Michele.

CHAPTER 23

Israel and Ethiopia

I was having second thoughts as I parked my car. "Larry what have you done? Why did you sell the business you loved to go to Israel to be a Director of a charity in a land with a culture so foreign to everything you know?" I was nearly knocked over by the heat. It's hardly ever hot in England, and I cursed myself for wearing a suit and tie. "For God's sake, this is Israel, and everyone is very casual." I removed my tie and made my way to the office where my new job as Director of Employment Services would begin.

In my new role, I would create eight job centres across Israel that would assist immigrants in finding employment and entering the job market. Most of the immigrants I worked with came from the former Soviet Union, refugees arriving with a couple of cases and the clothes they were wearing; and those coming from Ethiopia with even less. The work was fascinating and heart-breaking and every day I heard stories of the persecution and sacrifices these immigrants endured to make it to Israel.

The situation of the Ethiopian Jews was especially dire. Many had walked for hundreds of miles across the treacherous territories of Sudan to find a home in Israel. Many had horrific stories, including children who told me they had seen people slaughtered in front of them and others dying of fatigue and hunger on the long and difficult journey. The Israeli government responded with its famous airlift rescue operations like Operation Moses in 1984 or Operation Joshua in 1985. Additionally, Israel provided all the new immigrants with housing, initially in an absorption centre. Whilst the accommodation was basic, they were clean and safe.

Israel welcomed all Jews, no matter where they lived or their backgrounds. In 1950 the Knesset instituted the Law of Return where every Jew who expressed a desire to settle in Israel would be guaranteed citizenship.

I was invited by the Jewish Agency to go on a mission to Ethiopia and accompany families on their migration journey to Israel. What I discovered was that these people not only lived 2,000 miles away from Israel, but also 2,000 years away. On landing in Addis Ababa I was taken to the Israeli Embassy compound where the refugees who had obtained visas to Israel were undergoing an induction programme.

In the Embassy compound, there were approximately 30 men and women sitting in flowing white robes intensely listening to a lecture. On the platform in front of them were four items: a television, a refrigerator, a gas hob for cooking, and a porcelain toilet with a flush lever. The lecturer was explaining to them how a refrigerator worked, something they had never heard of or seen before. They also had never seen ice and, as a bowl was passed around, people were fascinated yet nervous to touch it. Next, the lecturer moved onto the gas hob which they would use to cook their own food. They learned how to light it. The lecturer then explained the danger of leaving the gas on without igniting the flame, using his hands and voice to animate an explosion. He then explained how a television worked, but there was no place to plug it in.

The most amazing part of the lecture was the explanation of the toilet. Most of the people came from areas by rivers, and there was no shortage of water when they wanted to do their ablutions. They were told to sit on a porcelain seat to do their business, and tear a piece of paper, and wipe it on their bottom, then drop it into the toilet before pressing a lever to flush away the waste. After, they were told to wash their hands in a sink. They were utterly confused. The problem with the demonstration was that the toilet was not plumbed in. I felt real stress on their behalf knowing how much adapting they would need to do.

The day came when we were to leave Ethiopia. It was 11:00pm, and three coaches pulled up to the embassy. 63 people with very few belongings sat in total silence, about to start their journey into a new millennium. What shocked me was that they had been given western clothes and, as they sat on the plane, I could not, again, get over how they just sat in complete silence. They had never seen a plane close up before, but there was an Ethiopian song that talked about the giant bird in the sky that would pick them up one day and take them to Israel.

The agreement between Ethiopia and Israel was that Israel paid money to the Ethiopian government to allow the Jews to leave, but almost always not as a full-family unit; mothers separated from children, husbands separated from wives. The Ethiopian government profited because Israel was willing to pay to get Jews out.

During the flight, I reminded myself that many of these people were about to be reunited with family members who had made the arduous trip to Israel, some of them years before. As the plane landed, and we disembarked, welcome crews began singing an uplifting rendition of a famous Jewish song: Shalom Alechem, Welcome / Peace Be Upon You, and handed out sweets to the children. They didn't know if it was something to eat or play with. I knew that behind those doors were waiting family members who hadn't seen each other in years.

I was provided with a video camera just for this occasion and began filming. As the doors opened, there was complete silence. Everyone, including airport staff, those on the mission, and the Ethiopians held their breath. In silence, mothers looked for their children and men looked for their wives. There was a rush forward as they recognised their loved ones and kissed and hugged each other for a very long time. My video never came out. The only noise came from the mission staff and me who were sobbing.

My time in Israel was marked with satisfaction. I was transforming from an absent father into a present father. Yet, it didn't come close to the happiness these families must have felt at that moment after finally being reunited with each other. To this day, I am proud that I had the honour of being a small part in helping these immigrants settle in Israel. Many have become doctors, lawyers, computer scientists, politicians, a backbone of the society that welcomed them. The lack of education and poverty many Ethiopians still experience cannot be ignored, and it will be many years before the majority can reach their full potential.

On one trip back to Tel Aviv from the Ethiopian absorption centre in Safed in the North of Israel, the staff and I were discussing the fact that many of the children were approaching Bar/Bat Mitzvah age. At some point, I ended up talking about my own miserable Bar Mitzvah experience. Sefton Bergson, UJIA Galil Programme Supervisor, leaned over to me and said, "Larry, I wonder how you would feel about creating a really beautiful Bar and Bat Mitzvah project for these children. I think it would be great if you would be involved with a whole programme that would begin a year before with educational and social activities. Now comes the exciting part; we will set up a twinning programme with kids in the UK."

It was July 24th 1997, the first twinning event and ceremony but it was more than just a ceremony. It was the culmination of a year of planning and preparation. The British twins would meet their Ethiopian twins at the absorption centre in Safed. I watched as the families of the British twins gave presents to their Ethiopian twins. It was humbling to see the expressions of wonder and joy as the kids opened their gifts. Three days later, I was standing with Michele and my family, along with other donors I had recruited, outside the Great Synagogue in Jerusalem awaiting the arrival of the Ethiopian kids and their families.

As the bus shuddered to a halt, we all rushed toward it. The doors opened and out they came, the men and boys in trousers and shirts and the women and girls in their traditional Ethiopian white robes with colourful turbans. Although it was a four-hour bumpy ride, they didn't seem tired at all. This was their first time in Jerusalem. Again, what surprised me was how quiet they were. No cries of adulation. No songs of jubilation. Just wide eyes and respectful silence.

There were 16 boys and nine girls from the UK who were twinned with the same number from the Ethiopian community. As we entered the Great Synagogue, these 28 kids and their families kept looking all around them in awe. The synagogue, modelled on The Second Temple, is grand and breathtaking with its stained-glass windows. It was that look in their eyes that gave away how entranced they were by what they were seeing. The boys put on the traditional tefillin that marks the day of becoming a man, and then the girls began walking in a procession as the cantor began singing Aishet Chayil, A Woman of Valour, composed by King Solomon. It was a beautiful moment, and I couldn't get over the fact that these brave people had travelled 2,000 miles and 2,000 years to celebrate their freedom in Israel.

About two months later, on an average Tuesday morning, I dropped by Michele's father's apartment to pick up his post. As I was walking up the stairwell, I passed an elegantly dressed woman on her way down. Suddenly, I turned around, took another look, and cried out, "Miss Silver?"

She turned, and it was her. It was really her! 35 years had passed but she still looked the same. Memories of Hebrew school, and the smell of the foisty classroom came back, yet at the same time the aroma of the chocolate bars she brought me as treats flooded in. "Miss Silver, it's me. Larry, Laurence Gould. Don't you remember me?"

She didn't. Though, it had been years since I was that eight-year-old student with a crush on her, she smiled anyway and still spoke with that sing-song lilt I'll never forget. She had divorced the rabbi from Belgium, moved to Israel, remarried, and raised a family. I excitedly told her about Michele, my kids, and what we were doing in Israel. She smiled gracefully and told me that I'd done well, but added, "Of course it is difficult to remember all of my students from such a long time ago." I was crushed. In a daze, I wished her a good day and climbed up the stairs to the apartment.

I stood in front of the door listening to her footsteps as she made her way down the stairs and creaked the front door open. As the door slammed shut, I stood there in silence. "Wow, I can't believe that just happened." Although her reaction to me was disappointing, at last, I was so 'over' Miss Silver!

CHAPTER 24

Stomach Pains in Thailand

We decided to take a family holiday to Phuket, Thailand. It was almost the two-year mark of living in Israel, yet Michele and I had not spoken about plans, because I could see how happy she was in Israel.

Whilst Israel is a modern country and a great place to live, thoughts of England had been tugging more strongly on my mind. I loved Israel's people and the sights, but culturally I was still very British. On our first day in Phuket, we went to the beach and laid in the sun looking out at the water with its turquoise waves. An Australian couple sat next to us, and the guy turned and said, "Ah, this is paradise, 'ey mate?" Michele smiled and raised her glass to her lips. "Yes, this is wonderful. Absolutely wonderful. Right, Larry?"

"Michele, do you remember how back in England, before we sold the business, I used to always get knots in my stomach?"

"Yes that's because you were always so stressed about work,"

"Well, I realise how much I *miss* those stomach pains. I hate these fucking palm trees. They just keep swaying back and forth, and this bloody ocean won't shut up with its never-ending waves. Michele, it was amazing to sell the business, it was wonderful to get all that money, and it's been incredible having our two-year adventure in Israel. But I'm itching, no, I need to get back to work, to work at something, to an overwhelmingly busy schedule and the relief of knots in my stomach. Can we please, please move back to England?"

Michele, just smiled and said, "Sure, Larry. Now drink your drink before the ice melts."

CHAPTER 25

Dealing with the Past

A week after returning from Thailand, I received a call from my friend Bryan Clarke inviting me to come to the US to discuss working with him. He was responsible for acquiring companies and then adding other acquisitions and he felt I could do a really useful job of bringing those companies together as a single entity. I told Michele, I'd like to check it out.

On the plane, I began thinking about how different this trip would be from the first time I had been in the States. "This time, I'm wearing a bespoke tailored suit that I paid for myself. This time, I paid for my own first-class ticket. This time I'm going to New York without anxiety about the future, rather with gratitude for the business built with my bare hands." I was satisfied.

Then my smug smile disappeared. Guilt washed over me as I thought about how I had treated Uncle Cyril. For the remainder of the eight-hour flight, I couldn't stop thinking about him, and I came to the conclusion that, for all my talk of liberation and independence, I had been an ungrateful brat.

My departure from New York and Cyril meant that I had lost my family's financial security, and my mother was cut off from her only family. Even when I had invited him to my wedding, it was a perfunctory gesture mainly done for my mother's sake. For me, all I cared about was the chance he might send a cheque like he had for my Bar Mitzvah. He replied with a short note saying he was happy for my success and wished me the best for the future. There was no cheque. I noticed on his reply card that he had moved to Long Island. I didn't care why.

As the plane descended and the lights of JFK greeted me, I didn't feel excitement like the first time. Two decades had gone by without reflecting on what had transpired between Cyril and me. As the plane landed, people began to applaud. I was feeling shame and deep regret. Uncle Cyril would have been in his late 80s and may not be alive.

Bryan picked me up in his limo. We spoke about our families, and he introduced me to his driver. Even though Bryan was one of my closest friends and colleagues in England, I was distracted for the rest of the ride to the Plaza Hotel. The bellhop whisked my luggage off to a King Suite, and Bryan and I made our way to a private booth at the bar to sip champagne.

But Cyril wouldn't leave me alone. I made up some excuse about jetlag and told Bryan I'd see him in the morning for breakfast. As I sat on the ornate bed and gazed at the lavishness all around me, I found myself dialling the operator.

"Hello Mr. Gould. How may I serve you?"

"Um, you know what, never mind."

"What the hell was I thinking?"

30 minutes later, I picked up the phone again. Within seconds of making my inquiry, the operator told me there was one listing of a Cyril Marcus living in Dix Hills, Long Island.

The operator made the connection, and I began pacing.

"Oh my God, oh my God, oh my God, it can't really be his number, it has to be someone else." A woman answered the phone.

"Celia?"

"Yes, who's calling please?"

"This is Larry."

She paused and then began to shriek, "Oh my God. Larry? Larry! Oh my God! It's really you! Hold on. Stay on the line."

"Larry! Larry! Where are you?" Cyril's voice was feeble.

This was not the reception I expected nor the reception I deserved. As soon as I said I was in New York, he joyfully continued, "Can you come to Dix Hills now?! I'll give you directions. Do you have a pen?" In classic Cyril style, he followed up with, "And does it work?" I told him I needed to rest, it was 11:00pm. I'd come first thing in the morning.

I hung up the phone and called Bryan to tell him I was cancelling our breakfast so I could see my uncle whom I hadn't seen in 23 years. Bryan told me his driver would take me.

I didn't sleep that night, mainly because Uncle Cyril kept calling me to check that I understood the directions. I told him I had a driver, but he kept telling me which trains to take and how I had to leave immediately. It was 2:30am. I reassured him I'd be coming out first thing in the morning and should arrive at his house by 9:00am. Five minutes later, he was back on the phone with some new piece of information he wanted me to write down to make sure I got there. This must have happened at least five times throughout the night.

In the morning, I called my mother from the limo and told her I was going to see Uncle Cyril. She was ecstatic. It took an hour to arrive in Dix Hills and, along the way, I told my driver the entire story from beginning to end.

At 9:04am, we turned the corner onto Cyril's street, Majestic Drive, and there he was. Smaller, thinner, and standing in the driveway. With his pyjamas flapping in the wind from under his heavy coat, he held up an umbrella as snow tumbled around him. It hadn't stopped him from waiting for me outside to arrive. I didn't wait for the driver to fully stop and flung open the limo door and rushed to Cyril. He held onto me for a long time.

Cyril married Celia a year after I left. They owned a large home with a huge garden. Antiques filled the halls, but were all covered with dust sheets as they were being sold because it had become too difficult for Celia to keep clean. I wasn't in the house for more than 10 minutes before he gave me the phone and told me he wanted to speak to my mum. It was very emotional to witness their phone call, and I felt really good. Uncle Cyril was overjoyed that 23 years later, she was still alive.

That night, Cyril demanded we go out to a fancy restaurant to celebrate. As the waiters seated us, Cyril turned to me.

"Larry, what do you want?"

With a smile, I responded, "Uncle Cyril, what do you recommend?"

He beamed and shouted, "OK waiter, we'll have three steaks, medium rare!"

Three weeks later, I brought Michele and our three kids to visit. Cyril was so excited to meet everyone, but really took to my youngest, Ilan who was an avid chess player. They'd sit for hours playing and talking animatedly to each other. For the next seven years, I made a point to visit him with my family as often as possible. I was so happy that the kids loved Cyril and Celia.

The last time I saw him, he was getting visibly weaker. Whilst we were sitting together by the fireplace, he turned to me, "Larry, I have no children. Celia, who is Catholic, has promised me that she will make sure I am buried in the Jewish way. I want you to promise that you will say the mourners Kaddish for me."

Kaddish is an ancient Jewish prayer recited in Aramaic by those mourning the loss of a family member. It is traditionally said by a male relative, usually, a son. As the fire crackled beside us, I told Uncle Cyril he needn't worry. I would say Kaddish for him and make sure he was buried in the tradition of our ancestors. He was so happy to tell Celia about my promise.

When I told my friend Maurice what I had committed myself to, he warned me that I needed to speak to my father to get permission to say Kaddish for Cyril. It was something about Kaddish being traditionally said by a son of the departed and how my standing in as Cyril's son in this regard might be offensive to my parents who were still alive. Of course, my mother said it was fine; but my father refused to give me permission and told me someone else should do it.

"Fine, Dad. I don't care so much about all this religious stuff anyway. But know this, if I don't say Kaddish for him, I won't say it for you either."

My father nervously cleared his throat. "I was only joking, Larry. You take everything so seriously."

Six weeks later, Uncle Cyril died. Celia made sure to tell me she was getting an Orthodox rabbi to officiate at the funeral, and I had to be there to say Kaddish. "Larry, you promised!"

When I arrived in New York, I immediately went to visit Celia. She was furious. "Celia, what's the matter?"

"What's the matter?! What's the MATTER?! I ordered a big fancy casket for Cyril and now the rabbi said that it's not kosher. We need a simple pine box."

"Oh, I'm sorry Celia. That's the traditional custom."

"I know. I know. That's fine with me. But what am I going to do with this casket? I called the undertaker, and he won't give me a refund."

"Well, you have a big garage. Maybe store it, and keep it for yourself?"

She calmed down, hugged me tight, and thanked me for the excellent suggestion. I spent a couple more hours with her and then excused myself to the hotel. I didn't tell her that I had never said Kaddish before and wanted to spend some time practising.

The next morning, I was sitting in the hotel restaurant and was about to order a special breakfast for myself: bacon and eggs.

"It's OK, I told myself. I've schlepped all the way across the pond to say Kaddish. God won't mind if I have a little pork to reward myself."

I opened the Kaddish prayer in front of me, put on my kippah and thought I'd get in a couple more practice runs before breakfast. As I was muttering it under my breath, a middle-aged waitress with a thick Brooklyn accent approached my table. In what seemed like an extra-loud voice, she joyfully called out for the entire room to hear, "Excuse me rabbi, what kin I getcha?"

I raised my eyes to Heaven, cursed Uncle Cyril, and ordered the fruit salad.

While I was eating and practising Kaddish, this Italian-looking guy with slicked back hair entered the restaurant. As soon as he saw my kippah, he sauntered over in pure mobster style. As I stood up, he shook my hand with a vice-like grip, "I'ma Tony, and I'ma sorry fa ya loss, and I'ma here to pick'a you up, OK Larry." It wasn't question.

Celia was wearing mink and dripping in diamonds. "I want to look spectacular for Cyril," she said as she sat next to me in the back seat and ordered Tony to head to the funeral home. The pews were packed by all of Celia's relatives, extended relatives, friends, their extended relatives, and me. The funeral director silenced everyone, and Cyril's coffin, adorned with a large American flag, was wheeled into the room. Uncle Cyril was in the American army and served in the Second World War.

Two of Cyril's army buddies began walking up the aisle, using their canes. After painstakingly making it to the podium, one of them pulled

The Making of Mr Irresistible

out a crumpled piece of paper and read a poem about Cyril joining the big army base in the sky. Then the other one pulled out a tape recorder. He fumbled with the buttons for a few seconds, and screechy music blared out. Since it wasn't Beethoven's 5th or Tchaikovsky's 1812 Overture, I had no idea what it was. I quickly realised that it was the American national anthem because everyone stood up and put their hands over their hearts. As these two old guys fought over the volume knob, I had to bite my cheeks to keep from laughing. Eventually, they folded the flag and hobbled over to deliver it to Celia.

The funeral director then said, "Ladies and gentleman, please leave the chapel and wait outside while Mrs. Marcus says goodbye to her husband and Mr. Gould says goodbye to his uncle. Thank you so much."

To my horror, they took the lid off the coffin and there was Cyril not looking so great, especially after being dead for three days. Celia was speaking to him, "My poor Cyril, my poor Cyril." The rabbi entered the room holding a terracotta pot which he smashed into three parts. I nearly passed out as he placed two pieces of the pot over Cyril's eyes and one over his mouth and then recited a prayer. He stepped back and Celia turned to me, "Larry, would you like to kiss Uncle Cyril goodbye?" I was trying not to throw up and somehow managed to spit out, "No Celia, I think it is important for you to have this final moment alone with him," and I shot out of the room.

As I closed the door on Celia who was softly singing a lullaby to Cyril, a hand grabbed my shoulder. I jumped out of my skin, but it was just the rabbi. He wanted to review the funeral service with me before it began and asked if I had any questions. When I told him I wanted to say Kaddish, he stroked his beard solemnly. "Well, Mr. Gould, this could be a problem. The only Jews at this service are me, you, and your dearly departed. And, in order to say Kaddish, we must have a minyan (a quorum of 10 Jewish men)."

A part of me wanted to yell at the rabbi, "Do you know what I gave up this morning for this?", but I was actually relieved that I wouldn't have to embarrass myself by stumbling over all those Aramaic words.

As we gathered at the cemetery, all of Celia's family and friends came over to me, slapping me on the back, hugging me, and sticking their faces into mine to tell me various versions of "Hey, I'm Joe or Vinnie". The Chabad rabbi did a marvellous job leading the service and explaining the steps of a Jewish burial to all the cross-wearing attendees. As I was thinking how odd this was, I heard my name called. The rabbi had invited me to say a few words. I wasn't prepared.

"Uh, Uncle Cyril loved three things. He loved being Jewish. He loved being American. And he loved Celia." A hundred Italians cheered.

Later that day, I attended Cyril's favourite Italian restaurant where Celia had arranged a wake for him. Celia's family toasted Uncle Cyril, gulped down copious amounts of alcohol and then hit the dance floor as Sinatra blared. This was a very different way of mourning than the traditional shiva (the Jewish mourning period of seven days). But I could tell it meant a lot to Celia that I was there. Actually, I kind of enjoyed it, and I was relieved I had been there for Cyril when we hadn't spoken for so long.

The morning after the funeral, Celia came to my hotel to meet me for breakfast. I was eating Special K. I had the same waitress, and she still thought I was a rabbi. "Larry, you have been like the son I never had, and you made the last few years of Cyril's life very happy, and I couldn't have gotten through these last days without you." She took a large manila envelope out of her bag. My heart skipped a beat. Maybe I was back in the will!

"I have gifts for the family." As she pulled out various trinkets, she spoke about how beloved I was to Cyril and how much I meant to the both of them. "Larry, I've got something for you." Maybe I was getting the Alaskan pipeline shares back or the deed to the house?! Celia paused dramatically and then pulled out a pair of cufflinks, Cyril's favourite pair. "He wanted you to have them." I told her I was overwhelmed, and I laughed at myself.

My flight home was the next morning, so that night I went to see Mama Mia on Broadway. There's a part in the show where everyone is dancing in the aisles to the song I Believe in Angels. As I sang and danced with those around me, tears rolled down my face, and I could have sworn I heard my Uncle Cyril say, "Amen."

Celia and I, along with Michele and the kids, remained close until she passed away in 2019. Shortly before, she gave Joshua Uncle Cyril's car, a 1993 Chrysler LeBarron, which he still owns. Although I wish things had gone differently between Cyril and me earlier in my life, I have never regretted leaving America the way I did. I do regret not having the awareness and gratitude for what he was trying to do to help me. If I could do it over again, I would have approached my departure with more tact and grace. But I still would have left, and I still would have renounced the will and Alaskan pipeline stocks. The feeling of liberation and independence I gained from breaking free of my golden cage was worth losing millions of dollars any day.

CHAPTER 26

Manchester Re-United

To my surprise, moving back to England didn't excite me in the way I thought it would. We originally planned to move to London which we felt would be a new adventure. However, at the end of the day, we chose Hale on the outskirts of Manchester, mainly because Michele's father, sisters, and their families were in Leeds, and my parents were getting older and frailer which made it easier for us to see them as it was much nearer than London.

Leeds had been a great place to live, but going back no longer appealed. When we did tell our friends and family of our decision, it went down like a lead balloon. Some friends said that obviously they weren't smart enough for us anymore. Another friend told me, "You're going to Hale because we're not rich enough for you." They all understood why we moved to Israel, but couldn't understand why, on our return, we chose not to live in Leeds. My parents felt let down that we were not going to live around the corner from them. I think Dianne was glad I was back in the UK, but was also a little perplexed why we chose Manchester.

Whilst we believed we hadn't changed, the attitude of many our friends certainly had, and we were no longer prepared to pretend this was

OK. I was still surprised by how a number of friends seemed irritated by my success. When we spoke about holiday arrangements for instance, they would respond, "Nowhere as expensive as you Larry." Depending on my mood, I would either become modest or go to the other extreme and show off because I was so irritated by these inverted snobs. I didn't like myself for letting them put me in that place. Perhaps my friends felt I was getting above myself, and maybe the wealth manager at Barclays had been right after all.

Before moving from Israel, I made a few reconnaissance visits to Manchester. The property market was hot, and I was getting desperate as this was my third trip and I had not had any success. Houses were being sold before I'd even landed. The agent told me that he had managed to get me a viewing, and I had the first appointment. There would be 12 other potential buyers after me, so if I liked it I would have to make a quick decision. It was a contemporary 1960s house, but really with only two great features. Firstly, it had a lot of windows and, secondly, one of the most magical gardens I had ever seen. I didn't even look at the house, I just stood at the window and looked at the garden. My heart was pounding. This ugly house had huge potential, and the garden was spectacular.

The doorbell rang, and the agent said, "That will be the next person for viewing." I told the agent that he needed to wait because I had to ring Michele for permission to buy the house. She was at the hairdresser in Herzliya. When she answered my call, I blurted out, "I've seen this house, and it's fantastic. I really, really, really want to buy it, it will be great for us, you will love it, so can I buy it?" She said, "Yes, please." Ten hours later when I arrived back in Israel, she claimed that she did say yes, but it was to the hairdresser asking if she wanted conditioner, and at that point the connection had been lost.

The day arrived when the Gould family returned to England, and

I began to panic. I knew that the house would be perfect once we had completely remodelled it; but as we approached the house, I had an awful feeling that Michele and the kids would not be able to see the potential despite the wonderful drawings that Simon, our architect, had made. I realised my big mistake was not having them sent to Michele before we arrived at the house. It was a perfect English spring day, sunny and warm with a gentle breeze. We stopped outside of 18 Broad Lane, one of the best streets in Hale, at a house called Mansart. "This is going to be our new home," I proudly announced. The children began to laugh. Michele began to cry.

"Daddy, tell me again. Why did you buy a super old and ugly house?" asked Dalya. I told her, "It will be the best house ever, and as soon as Simon shows you the plans, you will understand why." Even though Michele and the kids weren't convinced, Simon did a good job.

Two weeks later, we moved in. Over the next year we renovated the property, creating an almost entire glass house with a view of the century-old gardens. From every part of the house we could see the pond, fountains, and special palm trees that had been shipped in from Australia by the former owner. I had never seen palm trees in an English garden, let alone in rainy Manchester.

The transition to life in Hale was made slightly easier because living in the area, were two couples we knew. David and Jo Scorah checked in every day to see if we were OK. Maurice and Rochelle Miller were very good friends to us in Israel and, when we told them we were moving back, to our surprise they told us that they were also moving back to Manchester to take care of aging parents, and happily they found a house in the same village.

On the beaches of Phuket, I was so certain of my decision to return home. The kids were settling in well but Michele and I were finding the transition more difficult. We all had to start our lives over, and for what?

"Had I made a terrible mistake?" Michele had to cope with a new house, and make a new life for herself. She became happier when she began charity work for the Federation of Jewish Services in Manchester and became a magistrate, working in the courts in Manchester. Every time she returned home from court, we would argue about the leniency she applied to some of the judgements. She said the system was supposed to rehabilitate people, not just imprison them. We often didn't agree.

I had no real job. At least in Israel I was doing something, and I loved the time with the kids who were enjoying their lives there. I had dragged them all away from that so I could do what, exactly? I felt panic as I was coping with what many people would have envied. I had made enough money to live a good life, and I had no need to work. I was totally free and totally bereft.

I was 47 years old and had lost direction. The self-doubt and depression got so pervasive that I began to question if even selling my business to Michael Milken three years earlier had been the right move. I had my beautiful home and a new Bentley but this in some ways made me feel worse, apart from the momentary thrill of acquiring these assets. "Oh my God, what have I done? What am I? Who am I?"

The last time I had felt this down was when Michele's mum, Yvonne, had been diagnosed with terminal cancer, some 13 years ago. Taking on a lot more responsibility with the family, I found the stress terrible to deal with. My father-in-law had no siblings and an elderly disabled mother. He had a wonderful marriage with Yvonne, and he and Michele and her sisters watched this attractive and vital woman being ravaged by the cancer. My job was to be as supportive as possible to them all, but it had a real toll on me. I began to have panic attacks.

I would be in a meeting or making a sales presentation or just on my journey home when I would feel my chest tighten and find it difficult to swallow, gasping for breath. For a number of weeks I tried to hide it, but as the attacks became more frequent, I decided to go to my doctor. This was not the time for me to be weak, I needed to be strong and pull myself together. I told the doctor my symptoms, but this was 1987 in England and being referred to a therapist was unusual and always something to hide.

My doctor was very sympathetic, especially as she knew Michele and her family. She told me she would give me medication to calm me down. My mind flooded back to those early years when I was suffering with migraines and heavily medicated. I was silent for a moment, as I recalled the effects the medication had on me. "No Doctor, I don't want to take medication." She looked a little disappointed and hesitantly said, I could refer you to a grief counsellor, then paused and looked very uncomfortable. She coughed and said, "That's probably a bit premature." I decided I was wasting my time and got up to leave. Then she said, "I do have an idea. There is a doctor, and he is a proper doctor who practises hypnotherapy. He has had some success with people like yourself where he teaches them to self-hypnotise and in that way, it helps alleviate the feelings of panic."

"Great, I'll see him."

"Oh, one more thing," she added as I was leaving the room. "Maybe it would be helpful for you to have a paper bag with you so that when you hyperventilate it will help you to slow your breathing down." Two days later, I went to see Dr Padwell.

I told him that I was not coping, especially as Yvonne was in such a terrible state, had lost weight, was a terrible colour, and fading quite rapidly. I told him I was trying to be strong for the family but the panic attacks were increasing. Over the next hour, he showed me a number of techniques including how to slow my breathing down and how to take my mind to a different place and therefore reduce the panic. Dr Padwell said that this technique needed a lot of practice, and if I put the effort in, I would really see the benefits. "After this first session, as well as practising, I want you to fill in this form and bring back the competed form at the next session in a week's time."

The form had three headings.

1. What are you most worried about?
2. What do you think is most likely to happen?
3. What can you do about it?

When I returned home, I did tell Michele about the breathing and techniques the doctor wanted me to practise, but I didn't tell her about the list. It is a list that I kept for many years. My answers to the questions were as follows:

Question 1) What are you most worried about?
i)   My mother-in-law will die.
ii) Michele will be heartbroken.
iii) Family life will be miserable.

Question 2) What do you think is most likely to happen?
i)   My mother-in-law will die in the next few weeks.
ii) Michele will be heartbroken.
iii) Michele will be miserable for a time, which will affect us all for a time.

Question 3) What can you do about it?
i)   There is nothing I can do about it.
ii) Be supportive to Michele.
iii) Be loving, patient, and supportive.

As I reflected back to this event thirteen years ago, I decided it was time to not only revisit those breathing and mindfulness techniques but to also write a new list.

Question 1) What are you most worried about?

i) I'm not working, and I'll lose all my money.

ii) I will not be attractive to Michele as I am not vital and dynamic anymore.

iii) I will become old before my time, because I don't have enough to occupy myself with.

When I read the list, I was beginning to feel ashamed of myself. With everything I had, I still forced myself to go on with the answers.

Question 2) What do you think is most likely to happen?

i) I am not working and spending, so I will use up all my money.

ii) If I don't find fulfilment in work / life, then I will continue to feel unattractive.

iii) It will be OK because if I let go of something, I must replace it with something else.

Question 3) What can you do about it?

i) I recalled a book that I read by a famous psychiatrist, Edith Eva Eger. I remember keeping a note of this. "Yes I am, yes I can, yes I will." Therefore, get up, get out, and get working.

ii) Get up, get out, and get working.

iii) Get up, get out, and get working.

With that in mind, I decided to go and visit my sister and my office in Leeds and to start creating the list of all the things I could do about changing my present situation. The voices in my head were shouting at me, "Who are you kidding? You severely want your stomach ache back. You want to work. To hell with the risk. Larry, have more confidence in yourself. Get back on the waggon and stop moaning."

I still owned Link-Up Languages and my sister, who had worked with me from the beginning, had taken over running the business in my absence and had done a great job, with an annual turnover of approximately $350,000. As I sat in my office at Belmont House, it felt good to be at my old desk again. Sitting there, I really felt like I had come home.

My sister came into my office looking quite excited. "We have an interesting business opportunity." It was 2000, and the world was exploding, powered by the World Wide Web, which allowed companies, big and small, to sell their services around the globe. The value of internet companies was also exploding, and Dianne told me she was quoting for the translation of a website. Language was the final barrier to trading globally on the internet. Even with the best website, businesses could not communicate with customers in their own languages unless it was translated and localised. Dianne continued, "This is a real change for our industry, Larry."

"So what you are saying is that our small language company should join the internet dot-com boom?" It took more time for all this information to sink in but when it did, it was an epiphany. "Yes, yes, yes," I said out loud as my driver and I sat in a traffic jam. "Just think, Larry, you could have a dot-com company." In this short visit to Leeds, I had a new job and a new business, even though I already owned it. But now I really felt like I owned it.

By the time I arrived home, I had dozens of ideas for a new business name. Too excited to wait until I had finished my dinner, I explained my plans to Michele, and she helped me finalise the name that would become our business brand: thebigword.com.

I needed to work out how Link-Up Services could be transformed into a dot-com company. The first thing I did was to meet with Dianne and our Finance Manager, Alistair Nichol, the next day, to share my plans about the new name and new vision for the business. I paced up and down while talking. "Keep still and sit down for goodness sake," said Dianne patiently irritated. But I was on a roll. "Let's tear down all the Link-Up Services signs, put up new ones, thebigword.com, we need a new website, it's got to be irresistible, we need to translate and localise our clients' websites and processes, we need FIGS on our website ..." Alistair interrupted, "I thought that figs are something you ate." Dianne groaned, "No Alistair, it stands for French, Italian, German and Spanish." I just kept going, "We need public relations, we need a marketing plan, we need analysis of our major competitors, and we need market testing." By the time I had stopped, thebigword.com was born.

Within a week, we tore down the old monochromatic Link-Up Language Services signs around the office and hung up fresh, multi-coloured, thebigword.com signs in their place. The next thing was to envision what we could do to make our services irresistible. I began investing in technology, buying up a number of software tools while simultaneously creating a new multilingual website for thebigword.com.

In the early days, we made many mistakes. On my first business trip to the US for thebigword, I had a meeting with knee and hip replacement manufacturers, DePuy in South Bend, Indiana. I was very proud to show them our new website where I could demonstrate how we could provide a quote in seconds. However, our website wouldn't open on a Mac, which at that time was mainly used in the United States, one of our biggest markets. I was trying to demonstrate our product and was mortified and angry that we hadn't tested it. After cooling down, I realised this was part of the learning curve. My job as owner of the business was to build its infrastructure and enlarge its client base and make sure that things worked before we sold them.

In addition to increased sales efforts, I began buying out small translation businesses. There were thousands of language and translation companies around the world. Many were struggling with the dot-com boom, and my targets were "mom and poppa" companies whose owners generally were looking to retire, especially in this period of change. I offered a lump sum exit strategy, along with two years' commission on their customer sales.

I bought a company in London called Multilingual. It did not focus on written translations, rather their main business was interpreting and voiceovers which would expand our portfolio. I had signed the deal with the company and had taken on additional borrowings to finance the acquisition. Their offices were in the centre of London, and it was a very exciting time having an operation in the capital which gave us more credibility and exposure, especially with international clients.

Following this acquisition, I acquired eight other companies, including one in Beijing and Tokyo. We used those companies as suppliers, and to gain entry into the Far East market. The other acquisitions were around the UK, and we transferred their business into our Leeds and London offices.

Within two years, we grew from an annual revenue of $400k to over $4m. Investments in technology and acquisitions had eroded my own pile of cash which was running out at an alarming rate. Despite our growth, I actually had an annual loss of $750,000. Not a great result, but this was dot-com boom time where this seemed to be acceptable, yet it was a dangerous route to take unless one had substantial resources. Whilst I could see the opportunities, I could also feel the great dangers that were heading in my direction. If I couldn't get those losses changed to profits, I would have serious cash issues.

Since I had sold my recruitment businesses five years ago and, despite the top line growth of the language business, I still wasn't adding to my wealth. I was alarmed about our prospects and whilst I was happy to have my tummy ache back, I didn't want it to be so painful. For cash reasons, I was forced to sell some of my investment properties. The dot-com boom was showing early signs of becoming a dot-com bust.

I was doing a considerable amount of travelling, flying to our offices in Japan and China and visiting prospective clients in the United States and throughout Europe, which again, wasn't easy on Michele. I also felt the pressure to do something, anything, to alter the course of the business. I had spent the past four years pumping my own cash into it, and my old financial insecurity was creeping back. "What if you lose it all? How much longer can you continue to invest your own money? This just isn't sustainable."

My stomach ache was back in full force.

CHAPTER 27

Rich List & Private Equity

"We need more cash, either from more profits or outside investors," I kept saying to myself, "Otherwise we will not survive." Using the remaining cash from the sale of the business, I was putting myself in a very risky position.

Luckily, despite our losses, we did attract a number of investors based on our irresistible technology. It was 2000, and even with our $9m revenue, with losses exceeding $800,000, we were still able to raise $8m from our private equity company, Aberdeen Murray Johnson (AMJ), for a 30% stake in the business. This meant that the business was really valued at around $25m. Not bad for a business that was losing money, but at least investors saw the huge potential driven by the massive expansion of the internet and that the issues regarding fulfilment were being resolved.

AMJ set strict conditions on how the money could be spent and insisted on a fixed salary for me. It was fantastic to get the money, but it was also very challenging as I had to receive permission for any expenditure above $50,000. So despite being the majority shareholder at 70%, and the investors at a 30% stake, they had the power to veto me if they wished to do so.

In 2001, The Sunday Times published its annual rich list, listing me as one of the 100 richest people in the UK. I woke up to the phone ringing off the hook.

"Um, hello?"

"Larry! Larry! So good to hear your voice. I had no idea you were so rich!!"

"Um, who is this?"

"This is your old high school classmate, Leslie. Don't you remember me? Anyway, I have this new business I'm working on, and we're looking for investors, and I thought ..."

I hung up on him.

A second later, the phone rang again. This time, it was Janine, Michele's younger sister, "Larry, you've got to go out and get a copy of The Sunday Times. They're listing you on the "Rich List", saying you're worth more than $80m. That's not true, is it?"

I thanked her, hurriedly threw on some clothes and ran out to buy it. Sure enough, there I was on the "Rich List", clear as day. I immediately called my public relations guy, Eric Davidson.

"How is it I'm on the "Rich List" if I'm actually losing almost $800,000 annually? What the bloody hell is going on?" He said he'd make some calls. An hour later, he called me back. I hadn't left my seat. "Apparently, it is the interview you did with the Daily Telegraph when you announced the money you had raised from the venture capitalist firms. They asked you what you thought the business would be worth in the future, and they must have overestimated your value."

I was flustered, and he knew it.

"So how do we get them to retract it?"

"Can't do that. It's already out there."

"OK, what do I do to make this go away?"

"Nothing."

"Are you telling me that I pay you all this money, and you can't do anything about it?"

Always the professional, Eric calmed me down by talking some sense into me. "Look, even if you deny it, no one will believe you anyway, especially as you have sold out in the past. The best way not to bring more attention to this is not to bring more attention to this. That includes not denying it. Plus, it may even help with your reputation in the business sector and your ability to open more doors and raise more funds."

I knew he was right and begrudgingly endured the next few weeks of flowers, cards, and congratulatory messages from all sorts of people I knew and didn't know. But, thank God, a year later Eric got me removed from the list. What bothered me the most was the adulation I received for something I hadn't actually earned. If I did have that amount of money in the bank, I would have been thrilled by the accomplishment and attention.

On the day the list came out, I got a call from my son Josh. He was now 17 years old and working at the local delicatessen on Sunday mornings. "Dad, people here are telling me that you're on the "Rich List". Is that true?" I sighed, responded in the affirmative, and waited for the congratulations I was sure to receive. "So why the bloody hell am I working at this deli for £3 an hour?"

In 2002, we identified a company in Belgium we wanted to buy. It was a translation services company working with the EU, and we had assessed that this purchase could open up the EU Government as a potential client. All we needed was approval from the board at AMJ. We agreed on the price, got the approval, and bought bottles of champagne.

I was due to fly to Belgium the next day to complete the deal when I got a message that the manager of AMJ had been sacked, and the new manager wanted to pull out of the Belgium deal. We were now caught up in their internal politics. At that moment I knew this was the second partnership I needed to get out of.

thebigword.com was now doing relatively well, whilst the majority of the other 65 firms that AMJ were involved with were in serious trouble. At first, I was devastated, especially as I had to pull out of the Belgium deal at the last minute; however, yet again, it was the push I needed. I bought back my shares from AMJ at an extremely good price.

Just like when I returned to my office after breaking up with Richard, I held another meeting with my team. Once again, I wrote IRRESISTIBLE on flipcharts all around the room, and once again my team worked out how we were going to become the most irresistible language company in the world.

My stomach ache was back in full force, as I had wished for in Phuket. I was elated. Four weeks later, we landed our biggest client, IBM. This boosted our credibility in the international market and, a little while after that, we received our first $1m contract for language services from Union Bank of Switzerland (UBS).

UBS wanted equity reports and market updates from around the world that would be translated within one hour. I knew I couldn't turn away such a prestigious client. Our technology team created software that allowed us to automatically engage linguists 24 hours a day around the world. The service was irresistible, and we began attracting more new clients. For the first time in years, we were not operating with a loss but growing at a steady pace and making a profit.

By now, I had stopped looking to buy other translation services companies and began focusing on improving our website, automating our processes, and creating more irresistible technology. We began tapping into new markets such as automated telephone interpreting services. Additionally, we were picking up a number of face-to-face interpreting contracts with various departments in the British government. For these contracts, I was focused on the human component of the translators we were sending into the field.

We created a testing process to ensure the linguists could handle the job and then invested in training so each would be equipped to deal with the situation they found themselves in, whether it was telling a patient that they had a terminal illness, helping a counter-terrorism unit interview a terrorist, or transcribing stories of torture from refugees seeking asylum.

Whilst the linguists did have the experience, many of them that were from outside of the UK had not gained a UK qualification and were therefore unable to get work that they were qualified to undertake. In order to provide skilled linguists with the right qualifications, we partnered with Leeds Metropolitan University (now Leeds Beckett University) to co-create online distance learning modules which also gave the students course credits towards their degree.

We were also growing in the technical translation markets, working with pharmaceutical and computer science companies. Those contracts, as well, required the right linguist to be matched with the right job, and we devised new testing and training in these areas.

With the help of a Government grant, thebigword and Leeds Met created the online International School of Linguists (ISL). Nine years later, ISL is still going strong but is now an independent company, and I am pleased to see that they offer continuous development opportunities to the linguist community.

The university were so thrilled with the results they did something I never dreamt of; they asked me to accept an honorary doctorate. I was over the moon. On a gorgeous July day in 2011, I walked up to the stage wearing a dark cap and gown. I paused at the elegant wooden podium to survey the hundreds of graduating students and their families. Michele and the kids were in the front row, and even my father had come. I looked down at my typed notes and then back out at all the faces waiting for me to speak. For years, I had identified as the kid who had dropped out of school at fifteen. Yet now, not only was I receiving a doctorate, I was the keynote speaker at the graduation ceremony with over a thousand in attendance. I was terrified.

I could see myself reflected on the large screens set up for the ceremony, and I cleared my throat. I began by congratulating all the students, their families, and professors. Then I told them point-blank that we actually had very little in common since they had all completed their higher education whereas I was actually a dropout but still managed to become a millionaire. Parents began glancing nervously at one another, and I could see the uncomfortable looks on the university leadership sitting near me.

Ignoring their reaction, I left a long pause and continued, "I wish each and every one of you the success of your dreams. But, at the end of the day, you are not like me. You have something I will never have. I may have achieved my career dreams, but you have this great resource that we call education. You have a way of thinking and a lens through which to view the world that I don't have. So, I urge you not to waste this gift that I was never blessed to have. Use it wisely, for you are truly ahead of the game."

I saw the professors heave a sigh of relief. I saw parents proudly slide their arms around their children. And I saw my own father crying, tears rolling down his cheeks. That made my day.

CHAPTER 28

Great Retirement, Great Sex

The children were growing up fast, and my Dad began stopping by my office unannounced, again, with no real purpose. But now I could better tolerate it. Nevertheless, we still had rows.

Life was good, and I was even taking advantage of the long journey to Leeds. In the morning, from my chauffeur-driven car I would talk to our offices in Beijing and Tokyo and in the evening, I would speak to the US office. I also used the time to make phone calls to family and friends although the calls to my mother were becoming more difficult as her dementia was progressing. She was still good at pleasantries, but would never use my name, only darling or sweetie. My conversations that would have lasted an hour in the past now barely lasted five minutes. Another good thing about having to travel to Leeds was that I was able to visit her although I was finding the visits increasingly distressing.

Dementia is one of the cruellest illnesses, and my lovely mum who had suffered with MS for all those years was now suffering with dementia. Often she didn't recognise who I was, but continued to be welcoming and charming and would make odd comments about how sexy my shoes looked and that she was waiting for her parents to come and collect her. I learnt a lot at that time, and one of the things I learnt was trying to avoid the temptation of testing my mother's memory with questions such as, "Do you remember who I am? Who has been to visit you today?" It is tempting, as you want to test where they are, hoping naively that things have got better or at least not deteriorated.

Bizarrely, the saddest times were when she did recognise me, and we could have a normal conversation for up to five minutes and then she would lapse back as her memory became disconnected again. After those conversations I would have to find a quiet corner and weep as it would remind me of what we had lost. My father visited her every single day for the five years she was in the home, and I was amazed how he was content to just sit and be with her. I would say to him, "I think it's great that you are happy to spend all this time with her, when she doesn't know who you are." He would just say, "I just love being with my Joycey." To be honest, as sad as it was, the end was also a relief.

In the latter days of her life she was very agitated, and there were times when I would glance at the pillow next to her and for brief moments consider how easy it would be to release my mother from her anguish. Listening to my mother calling, "Help me, help me, where am I?" was my main motivation. But after relief came anger. Anger that she had had to suffer so much. My father had always claimed to believe in God, unlike my mother. I smiled when I recalled when she said, "If there is a God and I get to heaven, I will absolutely wipe the floor with him," and I hope she did.

I also used the time on the journey to Leeds to dictate my first book to my long-suffering Executive Assistant, Janet Batten. When I had returned from Israel, KPMG who had acted for me with regard to the sale of Link-Up had invited me to talk at three conferences to high net worth individuals. My slot at their conference was to talk about the emotional effects of selling one's business.

It was a scary challenge as I had been out of the country for a couple of years and out of the habit of public speaking, at least without an interpreter. There was something safe about making a speech in Israel as I allowed the interpreter to translate my words. Also in that time, I was representing an organisation that the audience could benefit from such as receiving grants. It wasn't hard for me to achieve enthusiastic applause.

As I entered the grand hall of the Institute of Directors in Pall Mall London, there were seated over 120 people, some of the most powerful and wealthy in the UK. Between you and me, I was wishing at that moment that I could disappear. Additionally, I had to sit through the whole conference as I was the final speaker. "Oh God," I asked myself. "Why have I chosen such a title for my speech? How am I going to carry this off?"

As I walked to the podium, I was shaking from head to foot. The screen displayed the following information: "Larry J Gould. How to sell your business and still have a great sex life!"

The previous subjects had mainly been about tax and where you should or should not retire to. The audience, mainly mature men in dark suits, leaned forward and seemed to look very interested as I shared with them my experiences and how I felt after selling my business.

The main theme of my speech was to reflect on how very interesting work can be, not just in the good times. Looking back, some of the greatest challenges, although stressful, were stimulating and exciting, especially when those problems had been solved. Also, the camaraderie, including battles with co-workers had gone. All the stress had gone. All the excitement had gone. Of course, for the first time in my life, I felt financially secure. I felt irrelevant; I'd lost contact with some very interesting and stimulating people. Yes, I could do things that I didn't have time to do previously or couldn't afford to do. In my opinion, people who have lots of hobbies are simply making up for not having a stimulating job (probably not a popular opinion). I might have gained wealth, but I had lost power, direction, and interest. It didn't make me feel very sexy.

I received a rapturous applause, and The Sunday Times carried the story. 'Millionaires warned. Selling your business can affect your sex life'. A journalist from the Sunday Times said that this topic would be excellent content for a book. I duly took the advice and wrote the book. Over a two-year period, I used my own experience, and my assistant undertook a great deal of research for me. As I am not a psychiatrist or sexologist, I rather overdid the research. I also widened the appeal by changing it from selling a business to the broader category of retirement. Whilst this has not been a best seller, I was probably too young to write it. But it was great to receive messages from many people telling me that the book had really helped them. This is not an advert for the book, but I think you should wait for the second edition at some point. I promise it will include less research and more sex!

One of the things I found most exciting about growing the business over the next 15 years was that we acquired businesses and opened various new offices around the globe.

China and Japan were huge markets for us, and in 2000 we had bought Mitaka in Japan as we were getting business from British companies translating English into Japanese, but not so much the other way around, with the exception of our client, Honda, who I would visit every year. There were two things I learnt, if you wanted to grow your business in Japan, you needed to have an office in Japan, and if you wanted to service a large client there, you need to be accessible to the client.

In view of this, we opened our own office in Tokyo which continues to flourish. The Japanese are incredibly demanding, more than any other culture we deal with. They are also very critical if anything goes wrong. However, if you show deep regret, and demonstrate the remedies and deliver on them, then whilst they would never forget, they will be loyal.

In Tokyo, the meetings with Honda would be lengthy, and whilst they didn't speak much English, it was impressive how they would write in English on a whiteboard. They were exceedingly professional buyers and wanted to understand all the details. After those meetings, I would be invited out for a meal and *karaoke*. If there is one talent I don't have, it is singing; but there was no way I could say no. On my second trip to Tokyo after a disastrous first outing at *karaoke*, I decided that I needed to be prepared. At Heathrow airport, I bought a CD Walkman. Sitting in club class, the steward shook me and said, "Please, please, sir, stop making that noise." I realised that I had been attempting to sing The Beatle's, "A Hard Day's Night," rather louder than I had appreciated.

In that period our business was really exploding, with offices opening in Germany, The Netherlands, Italy, Sweden, and Denmark.

CHAPTER 29

New York, New York

I had opened an office on Wall Street in New York City in 2005 and packed off Josh to work with a guy we headhunted from one of our major competitors. Whilst I was excited for Josh, sending him on this adventure at 22 years old, I didn't realise how much I would miss seeing him. Michele, with the best intentions, insisted that we give him space and not to do an Uncle Cyril on him. So we decided that apart from emails and telephone calls, I would leave a gap of at least three months before visiting the New York office.

Since the reunion with Uncle Cyril in 2000, my enthusiasm for the US had been reignited, and the kids were converts, however, Michele could not see herself living in America on a permanent basis. Dalya had initially planned to move to London after finishing university. At the last minute she changed her mind and decided to move to The Big Apple to join our business. Finally, our son Ilan, who was studying at university in Israel and had initially planned to stay there, also decided that he wanted to be in New York with his brother and sister.

One icy December night in 2012, I saw my life coming to an end as my car skidded across the motorway towards a large lorry as I was returning to Hale from the office. It was a miracle that my driver, Aydin, was able to get control of the vehicle and avoid hitting the lorry. I was truly shaken as I walked into the house. Michele was sitting and gazing, lost in thought. Instead of her usual welcoming greeting, she turned to me and said, "Larry, do you know what day it is?" "Of course, it is the 18th of December, and it is now 24 years since your mother passed away. I kneeled down, put my arms around Michele, and hugged her.

"My mother never lived to see her grandchildren grow up; and Larry, this is not going to happen to me. With three children now living in America, I want to go and live there. I want to move." From the look on her face, I understood that this was not going to be negotiable. I was shocked as this had been my dream and certainly not Michele's. A dream that Michele had strongly resisted, and now she was eager to make the change.

The problem for me was that as time had passed living in Hale, I was really loving my life in the UK. I had the best of two worlds, a wonderful life in the UK apart from that long daily drive, and I was very happy that I now had an office in Manhattan. Since it was expanding, colleagues and I frequently visited, and I had decided to rent an apartment on Central Park South, as it was more cost effective for us and our staff to stay there, rather than pay for hotels. I was happy and not keen to change the status quo.

Michele was not only missing the family, but as she often travelled with me to Manhattan, she was now understanding and loving the city. Michele had found it very difficult to leave Israel but had made a huge success of life in Manchester. Not only was she a Director of thebigword, she was a magistrate, had a large circle of friends and was also involved in a range of voluntary work. What she was suggesting was turning my life upside down. Now the shoe was on the other foot.

It was one thing making regular trips to New York, but something completely different to live there full time. Despite the common language, the cultural differences between the UK and US, especially in relation to business, was really quite a shock to me. What was also challenging was that my humour tends to be very British – sarcastic and ironic – and often this did not go down well. Sometimes Americans just looked confused, whilst others were insulted. I remember when Michele's friend Karen, who was originally from Newcastle, wanted us to meet her Upper East Side husband. So, off I went with great expectations of making my first new best friend in America. As we approached the door, Michele said half-jokingly, "Larry, at least at the beginning of the evening, don't be yourself, let them get used to you."

In the end what really sealed the deal for me was that I, too, didn't want to be so far away, and the thought of not being in contact with our children and our expanding family apart from digital communications was something I couldn't imagine.

With a mixture of excitement about moving to the US and sadness and regret that we would be moving from our home and the friends we loved, we put the plans into place. At the age of 61, I was ambivalent, and the impending move was a huge upheaval. This would often wake me in the middle of the night. Michele had always done what I wanted and now it was my turn.

I would also have a change in commute. Instead of the 120-mile daily round trip to Leeds, now I would be taking regular 7,000-mile round trips to Leeds. Perhaps, for many people, this lifestyle would be a nightmare; but although jetlag was sometimes a problem, I loved and still love the excitement of working in different countries. It is a real privilege to get into that time machine and experience so many cultures in so many places. Long may it last! I have been travelling internationally since the age of 27, and forty years later, I'm still doing it, albeit in a more luxurious seat.

We said goodbye to our beautiful home in Hale. For convenience sake, we bought a small apartment in Leeds city centre so I could cut out my long daily commute when I was in England, which was still half the year. Michele was now living full time in the United States. It took another 18 months to eventually find our dream home in the beautiful village of Quogue in the Hamptons. This created more travelling as I now had a 170-mile round trip to Manhattan, but I've always employed the most wonderful Executive Assistants and, due to modern communications, I am able to work with my current EA Rory Bickerton while I am anywhere in the world. Apart from the strain of sitting for long periods in various modes of transport, I find those times useful for thinking and speaking to friends and colleagues.

It was extremely challenging to make friends when we first moved to New York. I think it is a guy thing. I found it very sweet that my kids seemed concerned that I should make friends; however, it was disconcerting listening to them offer advice. Josh suggested that I do voluntary work, Ilan said I should join a synagogue and business groups. The most depressing suggestion was when Dalya said, "Hey Dad, why don't you go back to night school and improve your French?" All I really needed in that moment was for them to bloody leave me alone. "Why on earth did I come here?"

In England, I knew many people at events I attended and, if I didn't, it was because I was probably the speaker. I joined the British American Business Association, and my first event was at the British Ambassador's residence in New York. As I approached the door, I had the same fear that I had felt at 13 when Dianne had taken me to her youth group. I laughed at myself when thoughts went through my mind like, "Will anyone speak to me? What shall I do when I walk in? What if everyone ignores me?"

I walked in and headed straight for a waiter who was carrying a tray of wine. I took a glass of white wine and for about ten minutes I had that "I am looking for someone I know who should be here" look on my face. I left the hall and called our then Sales Director, Bernadette Byrne, who was great at networking. Thankfully, she answered the phone. "Bernie, I'm at this event, and I don't know what to do. I can't believe I have put myself in this position." She told me to stop being such a wuss. "All you have to do is go up to a group of people and say to them, 'Hi, my name is Larry Gould, and I've just come to live in New York and I have no friends. Will you please talk to me?'" "Bernie, you're joking?" "No, and if you do it, I won't tell anyone you made this call." It worked like an absolute charm.

I went up to four ladies and delivered my message. We had a wonderful conversation and exchanged business cards. Next, I headed for a group of three guys and used the same opening line. All three smiled and shook my hand. One of the guys held on and gave me an extra squeeze. Again, we had a good conversation and exchanged cards. I was feeling really good, and as I walked away the guy with the extra squeeze said to me, "I think we've really made a great connection," and put his hand around my shoulder. At that moment I stuttered, "Yyy … yes," and I made a quick exit. Michele laughed hysterically when I told her about my "making friends" evening.

After hearing this story, Dalya, who was my EA at the time, was particularly concerned that I should make friends in New York. I met a man called Simon Miller through Michele at a dinner party we had been invited to. Afterwards, he gave us some translation work, and Dalya suggested that I call him, thank him for the work, and ask him if he'd like to meet for a coffee or a walk. "Dad, I know you miss your walking friends in England. Why don't you ask him to go for a walk with you?"

I sat at my desk and prepared to make the call. Before I had the chance to pick up the phone, Dalya had called again to check that I was making the arrangements. I had the same nervous feeling as when I would set up dates with girls in London all those years before. "What am I doing? Here I am 61 years old, and I was having to pluck up the courage to ask some guy to go for a walk." It would have been funny if it hadn't been happening to me. "Why can't I just be satisfied with Michele, my children, and my colleagues?" I knew the answer. I had to work harder at my out of work life. So, I picked up the phone and called Simon.

After talking a little about work, I got to the point. "Simon, back in England, I used to meet up with my friends every Sunday morning for a walk, and I wondered if you were ever free?" He reminded me that he was divorced and only able to see his kids at weekends, but then said, "This Sunday, I am actually free. See you at 10.00am?"

"Yes! Yes! Yes!"

Sunday morning, it was pouring down with rain, and as I sat in the lobby of 240 Central Park South holding two umbrellas, one for me and one for my date. It didn't bode well for a walk in Central Park. As I waited for him, I thought about what I would be doing in Hale.

Each Sunday morning, I would walk with friends for a couple of hours, stopping for coffee and cake in the village. Our walks were full of noise as we discussed our families, business, even politics. Maurice Miller was the friend who had looked after me so well when I arrived in Israel and had become like a brother to me. He was a real entrepreneur and had created a tremendous spectacles business since returning to England. Denis Jacobson was the newest arrival from Dublin, a lawyer who had inherited a number of properties; and we would often jibe him about his inherited wealth, especially since Maurice and I had come from such poor backgrounds.

Then there was Ronnie Abrahams. Mr Cool. Mr Impeccable. He was a typical English gentleman, but beneath his very proper exterior, he was great fun and a wonderful friend. We would laugh, shout, insult, and berate each other, and then return home with smiles on our faces.

At least twice a week I would speak to my friend Graham Rubin who lived over in Liverpool. There is nobody in the world who can make me laugh like Graham. We both have the same sarcastic sense of humour. Graham had created a very successful online and printed catalogue company, and we would spend hours on the phone sharing ideas.

Oh, how I missed them all.

I was disturbed by the arrival of my date. "Hello Larry, do you normally walk with two umbrellas?" "Yes, in case I get tired." He didn't get the joke. I screwed my eyes up for a second and willed myself to be back in Hale when I opened them. I wondered if I needed the pressure of a play date with a serious American. I walked out of the building with both umbrellas. The ridiculous thing was that Simon had his own.

I was spending almost six months a year away from my wife, who I adore being with, as I travelled regularly to Leeds and our other offices around the world. I was loving it in the daytime, but often lonely for Michele at night. Sadly, during this period, my father was approaching the age of 90, and his health was failing. So at least I was able to spend time with him in Leeds. To be honest, our relationship hadn't changed. But I was proud of how he dealt with being diagnosed with lung cancer and how he insisted on looking after himself until two weeks before his passing.

I would visit him almost every day when I was in the UK; sometimes the visits were cut short as we would fall out over some trivial matter (in usual fashion) but there were good times. My father had a tremendous relationship with all his grandchildren, and I often used him as a mediator when there were issues with my own kids. He did this well. The difficult relationship that I had with him still continued; however, of course it was greatly tempered by the fact that I went to all his hospital appointments with him. I sat with him when he was told that the cancer was worsening and that he should prepare over the next few months for an end of life scenario. He was incredibly brave and determined to make the best of it.

During this time, I experienced some moments of real affection for him. However, even in his final moments he was very angry with me. The doctors were not allowing him to take liquids by mouth. As I sat at his bedside, he was desperately thirsty and begged me to get him a drink. When I asked the nurse, she said the best they could do was to rub a damp cotton bud over his lips. It was dreadful seeing him trying to bite the cotton bud to feel the moisture in his mouth. True to our relationship, he said, "You're bloody useless and can't even get me a drink."

After saying this, he just seemed to look different, so I called the nurse. She turned to me and said, "I'm sorry Mr Gould, your father has passed away." With that she began to pull the cover over his face. "Hold on," I told her, "Please don't cover his face yet, and please give me a few moments by myself." She quickly left the room. "Dad, this is not the best way to end, so I am telling you that I hope you find peace, and if there is such a thing as heaven and mum's parents are there, please don't start arguing with them. Please find peace." As much as we had a lot of anger for each other, we also had love. I kissed him and covered his face.

Do I miss my father? To be honest, I really don't. But I have been left with a stronger feeling of affection than I thought I would and a deep admiration for his strength, and love for his grandchildren and theirs for him. I didn't need to find peace by forgiving him, rather I found it by understanding him. In fact, writing this book has given me the greatest opportunity to understand my father, which in itself was worth the effort.

CHAPTER 30

The Sale?

B y January 2018, thebigword was one of the top 20 language technology companies in the world. We were regularly being contacted by private equity companies or competitors who wanted to buy the company. One particular organisation was quite persistent and, I admit as I was approaching my mid-sixties, I did feel that I was missing being with Michele more, and she was missing the holidays that I promised her. Perhaps it was time to consider a deal. I talked to my advisers, and they suggested that I should put it out on the market and not just negotiate with one company to ensure the best price. The process began.

It involved sending out CIMs (Confidential Information Memorandums) to interested parties which gave a great deal of information on the company. On receipt of the CIMs, investors would decide whether to take it to the next stage. Over a period of six weeks, we began to collect expressions of interest. We then invited the companies that had made an indicative offer in an acceptable range to visit our offices. We then whittled it down to three offers and, after strenuous negotiations, I finally accepted the offer from one private equity company.

It was a very challenging time, of course. The Directors of the company and senior management understood the process we were going through. Naturally, there was a fear of the unknown but at the same time they would receive a substantial bonus and a share option scheme. For me, it was extremely difficult as my mind would wander back to the memories of last time I sold my business. This time, even though I was 23 years older, and happily 40 pounds lighter, full of energy, and loved my business more than ever, I still had that old anxiety about needing to consolidate my financial position. The business was doing well, but what if there was some great event or disaster, that through no fault of our own could destroy my business? My real wealth was mainly invested in thebigword. A little voice was telling me it was time to de-risk my wealth by selling.

The closing date to finalise the deal was in the second week of January 2018. The plan was that I would fly to Leeds the week before and sort out any outstanding negotiations, and Michele would join me a week later where we would sign the deal. During this period, I felt thoroughly depressed. If I had still been living in the UK, I would have received a number of offers to be a non-Executive Director of companies, as I had in the past. I had never taken up these roles as I wanted to focus all of my attention on thebigword. I was also regularly asked to speak at events around the UK, including radio and television.

However, after the sale, I would be based in the US, where I was unknown and with very few business contacts. My quandary was where to reinvest my money, how to gain invitations to speak, or to join any boards. It would be challenging. My fear wasn't because of my ego, or maybe it was. "Who am I now? How would I spend my time? Who would I be? I like my life. Do I just want to change it because I would be safe in the knowledge that Michele and I would be financially secure, and our kids would be too, for many years to come?"

In all these deals, there are always last minute negotiations, and finally I went with my adviser to a meeting with the buyer to iron out some organisational details which would include a discussion on the future of the management team. Speaking with Michele the night before, I told her that I really felt in my bones that it was a bad idea to sell. Her response was something along the lines of, "Oh, that's a surprise; I never thought we'd get this far." I entered the office, and the prospective buyer talked about the money they would invest in the business and discussed their thoughts on my team. But midway in his sentence, I put my hand up and said, "I think you are great, and you are a very professional team." He interrupted me and said, "Larry, you're going to enjoy this journey, and we will want you to be a non-Executive Director as we still need access to your great knowledge."

He mentioned that we had a great team but there would need to be some changes. I agreed with his comments. He seemed relieved with my response. I said there was just one last thing. "I am not selling the business." "Pardon?" "I'm sorry, I am not selling the business!" In the lift down to the lobby, my adviser, Paul Mann, couldn't believe I was punching the air in jubilation.

"Yes, yes, yes!"

As we went back to my office, plans started forming in my mind on how to reshape the business. I knew that I needed to appoint some new blood to my board and say farewell to those who had done a good job in the past, but I didn't believe would take us to the next stage.

Of course, the first job I had to do was to ring Michele and the children to tell them the news. Michele was totally unsurprised and unmoved, and I was pretty sure that the children felt somewhat disappointed but relieved at the same time. Money and security is very important, but I think too much of both is not good for motivation and can be bad for the soul. Speaking for myself, I felt rejuvenated and couldn't wait to get back to work and those stomach aches.

CHAPTER 31

Irresistible Consultant

16th May, 2019. I was woken by Michele as she opened the electric blinds of our bedroom, in Quogue, in the Hamptons. The sun light was flooding in, and I was irritated as I wasn't able to get to sleep until the early hours of the morning. With a cappuccino in hand, she began to sing happy birthday. Then I remembered why I couldn't fall asleep. It wasn't like when I was child because I was excited about presents I hoped to receive, but because I had been thinking about my future and also reflecting on how appointing a CEO to replace me had affected the business and my life.

Nothing is more irritating than when people say to you that age is just a number, which is, of course, bullshit. If you are 20, you sort of hope you will live to at least 80. But I had just turned 67, and 80 was just 13 summers away. Dangerously close. Although, I did take some solace from the fact that my mother, despite her MS, lived until she was 83, my father and one grandfather to 92, and my paternal grandmother to over 100. We'll leave Nana Cross from the list for obvious reasons.

Life really had changed for me. Despite being Chairman, and the fact that I had appointed a CEO in the previous summer to take care of the day-to-day running of the business, I had still continued to work full days and was still travelling a lot. This meant that the plan wasn't really working. We still had not found the time to take trips for pleasure. However, Michele was putting pressure on me and had already made bookings for a number of trips including Thailand, Mexico, and Colombia, and others remained on our bucket list. Whilst this was appealing, I had just not felt confident on easing back on the business. It was something that concerned me and disappointed Michele. I didn't feel comfortable letting go. Despite appointing a professional and experienced CEO, I could not let go of the reins, which I am sure was as much of a frustration for him as it was for me.

In the book I had written on a great retirement and how to still have a great sex life, which I wrote when I was 44, I had interviewed many retirees and the strongest suggestion that I learnt from the retirees was that you need to plan not only your finances, but the biggest mistake many admitted was that you need to plan how you will spend your time. So, I had to begin doing that.

With that in mind, whilst the new CEO who came from outside the industry had done some great things, I believed that now my son Joshua, after sixteen years working together, was more than ready to take over the job of Group CEO. Until that time, he had been the CEO of our defence company, TBW Global. He had done a brilliant job of growing it. I knew if it was to work with him as CEO of the Group, he had to have real autonomy, especially from me.

At the October board meeting, I announced Joshua's appointment. I have to admit I did sound out the board members prior to the announcement as I wanted to know that he would have their backing and was delighted with their responses. However, my next announcement did surprise them. Not only was I continuing as Chairman, I was adding a further title to my role: Irresistible Consultant.

The board and Josh looked perplexed. It is always difficult to step away and rather than me interfering with the day-to-day running of the business, like any consultant, I would propose to the board various projects that I would work on. At the same time, committing myself to delivering irresistible results placed quite a pressure on me, especially as I needed the board's buy-in before I could start a project. Acting as an Irresistible Consultant, in fact, created boundaries. The board now had control of the projects.

With more time on my hands, I began teaching at Cornell Tech University in 2019 where I have the privilege of working with post-doctoral associates who are on a runway programme created for academic entrepreneurs. I love the sessions I am doing with them on, yes, you guessed it, "How to Build an Irresistible Business". The programme is focused on sales and marketing, helping the associates in the art of creating an irresistible story around the products and services they have produced. These brilliant people are bringing a range of products and services to market which can be quite life changing; however, the gap that I see is that their experience with selling and marketing is limited. It is wonderful to see these talented people become real entrepreneurs.

I also now have more time to spend with my family and to travel. But I still continue to be fully occupied, as my EA, Rory, will testify.

CHAPTER 32

Not Really the Last Chapter

16th May, 2020, and I was woken up after a relatively peaceful night's sleep with a cappuccino, the electric blinds open, and Michele singing happy birthday to me.

My seventh grandchild, a boy, Enzo Julian, was four days old and, due to the Coronavirus, Michele and I had spent the last nine weeks socially distancing in Quogue. Nine weeks, just the two of us, and I loved it. Although, to our great disappointment, we were not allowed to visit our son Ilan, daughter-in-law Daniela, our granddaughters, and the new baby. It was a real blow. Thank goodness for video conferencing, which enabled us to be digitally present at our grandson's baby naming and brit. It was a very emotional moment as we were also joined by our family and friends around the world.

Covid-19 has been in some ways a disaster and ironically in other ways has introduced us to some great opportunities for the future. thebigword team, globally, had to react quickly to the changes forced by Covid-19. It had been an incredible challenge to our workforce and, despite the difficulties, thebigword team worked tirelessly to ensure the ongoing success of the business. They were superstars. The first few weeks were very scary, but with the technology in place, and support from the UK and US governments, we made excellent progress.

On 1st April, 2020, the business reached its 40th birthday, and I believe I am the longest serving Director in the top 50 language companies in the world who has full control of the shares. A few days after I appeared in the Sunday Times rich list, which was, of course, in error, I was contacted by a journalist who wanted to interview me about how I had grown the business. The last question he asked was, "What is your exit plan Mr Gould?" I have never believed it is a great thing to spend time thinking about how you are going to give something up. So, I gave him my honest answer. "It is my sincere hope that I die on my board room table!"

The COVID pandemic is the latest drama in my life, and there have been times when I have felt moments of panic. "Will somebody I love get ill? When will I be able to see my family? What is going to happen to my business?" I have also experienced moments of cabin fever. Being in one place for a long period of time is just not in my DNA.

On 8th June, 2020, the Governor of New York announced that shops and stores were allowed to reopen, providing only one person or family enter at one time Michele and I were so excited. It wasn't because we needed to go shopping, especially as buying online is the new normal. Though, I have to say, it is exciting when parcels are delivered to our house.

Michele said, "Let's go out and celebrate. Where do you want to go?" Without hesitation I replied, "Michele, we are going to the ice cream parlour." It was great to see that the tapes covering the benches on the street had been removed. I just wanted to sit down and enjoy an ice cream cone. With great anticipation, I entered Shock Ice Cream on Westhampton Main Street, of course, with my face covered. I was warmly greeted by the owner, Elise. She said, "Seeing you here is

Larry J Gould

reminding me that life is returning to some normality. Would you like your usual cone?"

"Yes, but this time with extra chocolate sprinkles and any extra toppings you can fit on without it toppling over." With great care, I ceremoniously walked to a bench and inhaled that tasty, creamy, smooth texture. Of course, it was so high that half of the ice cream fell onto my nice clean pink shorts.

I didn't give a damn. Linda Malkin, I was in heaven.

POSTSCRIPT

I was inspired for three reasons to write this book. Firstly, it is the 40th anniversary of my business. Secondly, I wanted my children and grandchildren to know more about our family history, and lastly, I was inspired by my journey back to Eastern Europe. From my research through Ancestry.com, I discovered all the small towns and villages where my family came from.

Investigating what happened to the Jews in those places, I learned that most were killed or driven out by the locals or sent to Nazi death camps. Those who survived ended up in the UK or the US, where the majority created new and successful lives.

As I grew up, I was often troubled by the stories of their suffering, but perhaps it was their suffering that impelled me to deal with my own failures. These survivors constantly reminded me how lucky I was despite some of the very difficult experiences I had.

To those who came before me, I also dedicate this book. Even in these difficult times, I am grateful to and appreciate how the UK and US created an environment where we could all flourish.